A **HOLIDAY** MAGAZINE

TRAVEL GUIDE

BRITAIN
ENGLAND, SCOTLAND, WALES

A HOLIDAY
Magazine

BRITAIN

England,

Prepared with the cooperation of the Editors of HOLIDAY

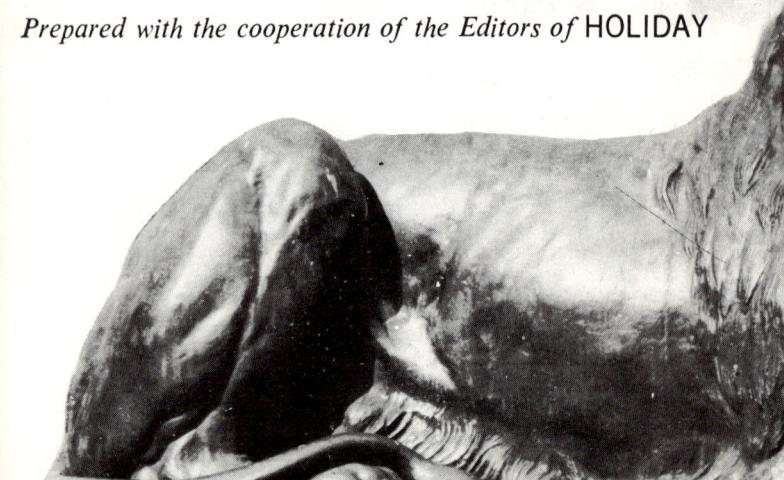

TRAVEL GUIDE

Scotland and Wales

RANDOM HOUSE
NEW YORK

© Copyright 1960, 1964, 1966, 1968, 1971, 1973 by THE CURTIS PUBLISHING COMPANY. All rights reserved under International and Pan-American Copyright Conventions. Published in New York by Random House, Inc., and simultaneously in Toronto, Canada, by Random House of Canada, Limited.
ISBN: 0-394-48450-9
Library of Congress Catalog Card Number: 72-11389
Manufactured in the United States of America

CONTENTS

CHAPTER

1 THIS IS BRITAIN 7
An island and her people, as familiar as Shakespeare or Dickens. Welsh, Scots, and Englishmen.

2 THE BACKGROUND OF GREAT BRITAIN 13
The ever-present past—that history which haunts the castles, towns, and villages and made the Britain of today.

3 WHAT YOU SHOULD KNOW ABOUT BRITAIN.......... 25
Preparing for your trip. Money and tipping. Transportation. Pubs and inns. Food, clothes, entertainment, and sports. Historic homes.

4 WHAT TO SEE IN ENGLAND...................... 49
A comfortable guide for finding your way about England. London. Heading south. Shakespeare and the midlands. The north country.

5 WHAT TO SEE IN SCOTLAND AND WALES 89
Highlands, lowlands, and the Scots. Edinburgh. Discovering Wales.

6 FACT FINDER 109
A selected list of hotels, inns, and restaurants in the cities and villages along your way, categorized by price.

CHAPTER *1*

THIS IS BRITAIN

Going to Britian is in some ways like going back home. Chances are that you will not have the feeling that you are seeing the country for the first time even though you have never been within a thousand miles of Big Ben. When you get to Britain, you are likely to feel that you are returning to a place you have known for a long time.

In a sense, you really have. Ever since you first heard that London Bridge was falling down, or met Doctor Foster on his way to Gloucester, or rode a cock-horse to Banbury Cross, you've been assembling some sort of picture of Britain. You couldn't very well avoid it. If you are like most Americans, you explored Sherwood Forest with Little John and Robin Hood, roamed the Highlands with Sir Walter Scott and Robert Louis Stevenson, rode merrily to Canterbury with Chaucer's company, visited London again and again with Dickens and Dr. Johnson and Pepys and Sherlock Holmes. Before you were out of your teens, you had the outline of your picture, and by now you have probably filled in more of the details than you realize. It is not at all surprising that from your first day in the British Isles you are likely to feel that you are among old friends.

You can hardly expect that your picture is always going to be precisely accurate. It may, in fact, be considerably out of focus sometimes. Take, for example, the matter of size. Most Americans have grown up with a sound respect for the British Empire, a firm appreciation of the resounding history of Britain, and a vivid (though sometimes vague) idea of London, the world's greatest metropolis. When they get to Britain, they are sometimes surprised that the country doesn't seem to be big enough to fit its history and

Trooping the Color at the Horse Guards Parade

"His land, his garden, his village . . ." Ross-on-Wye, Herefordshire

its achievements. Great Britian *is* small. All of it—England, Scotland, and Wales—adds up to no more than 88,000 square miles, a little less than the area of Oregon. Yet packed into this tight little island thrust out from the coast of Europe are 50,000,000 people, almost forty times the population of that state. For people who have been used to the vastness of the United States it is perhaps natural to be surprised that Britain is smaller than they expected. But there is another way to see it. It is even more astonishing that so small a nation could have produced so much.

It is true that the cultural heritage of America is the result of the blending of many diverse elements. But Britain was the mother country and our foundations have always been solidly British. It is easy to forget that the great tap-roots of what we call western culture so often lead back to this one tiny spot on the globe. The language which America shares with Britain—consider the incalculable influence of the King James Bible and Shakespeare alone—would have been sufficient to maintain the family bond. But America has borrowed freely from British sources in almost every other important area. The folklore and the legends which color American thought, the concepts of individual freedom, the basic political and social system, the concepts of right and justice, economic theory and the system of industrial production, the dominant Protestant outlook, the ideals of equality and service and achievement—all of these fundamental and decisive elements were developed in England and flowed from there to the New World. The great wonder, surely, is that one people and one small country could have contributed so many of the basic elements that have moulded the modern world.

Rural England: Tewkesbury Abbey, Gloucestershire

This Is Britain 9

The contrast between Britain's size and her achievements is only the first and most evident of the contradictions that you will encounter. Here, if ever there was one, is a country of paradoxes. For centuries Britain has been the center of the financial and banking world, yet this intricately organized and highly industrialized complex cannot feed its own population without imports. Britain is one of the few remaining monarchies in the western world; her people, staunchly and even militantly democratic, are at the same time profoundly loyal to their Queen. Though Britain is chief among the nations of the Commonwealth, the sovereignty which she exercises over Canada, Australia, New Zealand, Ghana and the other members is only symbolic. Once the foremost imperial power of the world, she has divested herself not only of empire but also of the will to dominate, and by doing so has won new and vigorous loyalty. Democratic by choice and by tradition, she is still capable

The Country House: Audley End, not far from London

of countenancing a society based frankly on class distinctions and at the same time of devising a political system with many of the attributes of the welfare state. Paradoxes on every hand, but all somehow absorbed comfortably within an indefinable unity.

In a way the Briton himself seems to have retreated before these contradictions. Far more than most people he values individuality. While Britain rose to world power and eminence, his interest remained firmly rooted in his own piece of land, his garden, his village. To others he may sometimes seem insular, even parochial. The fact is that he retains an abiding loyalty to what is near and close to him. The North Briton has never quite learned to be at ease with the people of the South. The Welsh and Scots still try resolutely to

10 Britain

keep their ancient languages and folkways alive. And everywhere the past is cherished and preserved.

The right to privacy and personal freedom is unquestioned by the British. Perhaps it is the lack of space that has fostered and maintained their fierce individualism. Good manners—even, perhaps, rigid formality—become necessary protective devices when neighbors are too close. But patterns can also become restrictive, and the Briton commonly looks for an escape. The city dweller turns to the country and to nature. He becomes an avid walker, he escapes happily to the countryside at every opportunity. The miner turns his tiny blackened yard into a garden, the surgeon becomes a proficient bird watcher, a fierce protector of all furred and feathered creatures. So deeply does he immerse himself in his private interest that he sometimes can seemingly quite ignore the fact that the world is rocking precariously—so long as it does not disturb his favorite nesting plover.

The British landscape itself seems to have been designed to encourage this diversity and individuality. Packed snugly together are lowlands and highlands; fen-country and hill-country; rolling green farms and gray, desolate moors. As an American you are long accustomed to contrasts in landscape, but you will hardly be prepared to find such extremes within an area no bigger than a middle-sized state. The British happily point out what an advantage it is to have such variety always at hand. The distance from the northernmost tip of Scotland to the southwest jut of Lands End in Cornwall is less than a thousand miles, and no part of the island is more than seventy-five miles from the sea.

Sulgrave Manor, home of George Washington's ancestors

Devon—daffodils, in masses, are the sign of spring in England

In the United States the people and their language remain essentially the same from one end to the other. Even continental distances produce nothing more startling than minor regional differences. But not in Britain. The very counties seem to be countries. There are many places in the world where you can cross national borders without encountering the contrasts you will meet on a drive from a village in Devon to one in Lancashire. Everywhere the differences in the people are emphasized by differences in their language. You are familiar with the Scots burr, you know that Welsh is a fathomless thicket of consonants, and you expect to find Cockney fast and difficult. But you can well be forgiven if you are not prepared for the perplexities of the Somerset dialect or find yourself defeated by the special vocabularies of Yorkshire and Northumberland.

But even though the details may be new and sometimes startling, all of this *is* the Great Britain that you have always known. It is the reality beneath all of the symbols you have ever learned—Piccadilly and Mother Goose; John Bull and Oxford don; the bobby, the barrister, and the Angry Young Man; the Cliffs of Dover and the fogs of London; the Scots fishermen who go out to the Banks and the Welshmen who go down the pits; Buckingham Palace and the Dickensian pub with the odd name and the pretty bar maid.

This is Great Britain, forever familiar and yet always new—the only country you can go back to before you have been there.

CHAPTER 2

THE BACKGROUND OF GREAT BRITAIN

Great Britain has no official birthdate. During the great civilizations of Egypt, Assyria, and Greece, Britain was only an outgrowth off the northwest coast of Europe. At a time when there had been no English Channel, various primitive tribes of Celtic character (such as Iberians and Basques), wandered over from the Continent and settled there. We depend on the tenuous findings and conjectures of archaeologists to inform us that these people were more sophisticated than cave-dwellers, that they were governed by a priestly class of Druids, worshiped the oak and the mistletoe (thus we unconsciously salute them at Christmas), and erected a number of perplexing stone monuments, of which Stonehenge is the most popular relic.

Recorded history of Great Britain begins about 55 B.C., when Julius Caesar landed on the south coast with his troops from Gaul. In his memoirs, Caesar described the Britons as a ferocious people, dark-haired, painted with blue woad dye. He had good reason to remember their ferocity: after two landings he was repulsed and driven back to sea. Not until a century later, during the reign of Claudius, was the conquest accomplished, and even then it took nine years. The unorganized tribes finally gave way to the civilized power of Rome.

Then the Roman colonists began to pour in, and, for four centuries, they lived there, exploiting the resources of the island for the glory (and profit) of Rome. The conquered people were not entirely docile, for we know of at least one unsuccessful revolt in 61 A.D., led by the tribal queen Boadicea. Like the American Indians in a much later century, the Britons practiced sporadic guerrilla warfare. But the Roman machine rolled over these disturbances, and gradually the colonists built towns (such as Colchester, York, Lincoln, Chester,

The mysterious Megaliths of Stonehenge

14 Britain

and London), erected villas, temples, bathing establishments, roads, and eventually brought Christianity to the island. There was little assimilation: a good number of recalcitrant Britons fled to remote parts of the island, such as Cornwall and Wales. Those who remained lived side by side with the Romans, the one in his mud hut, the other in his brick or stone house complete with central heat.

At this remote outpost of their empire, a corner where lines of communication were stretched thin, the Romans had to contend with marauders, particularly those from the north called Picts, a people of uncertain origin. The typical Roman solution was to build a wall across the waist of the island (from Newcastle to Carlisle), and for a long time this served its purpose. But the Roman Empire itself was in decline. Troubles at home and in the provinces meant that the forces in Britain had to be continually reduced. The Picts stepped up their incursions as the number of occupying troops diminished, and to add to the pressure, Saxon pirate ships began harrying operations from the North Sea.

By 406 the realistic Romans knew that the time had come to pack up and go back to dying Rome. Their leaving cut off the Britons from the Continent, and a number of years were spent in darkness, tribe fighting against tribe.

The end of this anarchy came in the middle of the 5th century, when a new conquest began. This time it was the blue-eyed, fair-haired Teutons (the Jutes, Saxons, and Angles) who made their bid for the island. These people came not as conquerors and exploiters, but as settlers, with no intention of pulling out when the going was hard. It took them nearly a hundred years to establish themselves, for the Britons savagely resisted them, too. Legend has it that the famous Arthur led one such attempt.

The reputation of the Anglo-Saxons as barbaric warriors with rolling eyes and wild beards is not wholly deserved, even though they were ruthless in their conquest. They brought with them a fairly advanced language, a rudimentary concept of law, a respect for family life, a deep-rooted pagan religion, and agricultural know-how. Their epic hero was Beowulf, a warrior who also was a gentleman.

True enough, they suppressed what Christianity the Romans had left into isolated flickers (with no less zeal than the Crusaders later showed in trying to stamp out Islam), and while they developed their island society, they had no real contact with the outside world.

But the outside world returned in 597, when Augustine, the missionary sent by Pope Gregory the Great, landed in Ebbfleet (Kent) and marched with banners flying to Canterbury. This non-military conquest of the island made headway slowly and against great odds; by the beginning of the 9th century, however, several of the British chieftains (now called kings) had been converted, and in 825, when the heathen King of Mercia was roundly defeated by the Christian King Egbert of Wessex, Christianity had a firm hold in Britain.

The Background of Great Britain 15

The increasing influence of the Church and a new outside threat began to unify the various factions. The seafaring Vikings (or Danes) had invaded coastal areas in the northeast, and the Anglo-Saxons, under the leadership of Wessex kings such as Alfred, set out from their capital in Winchester to repulse them.

During two centuries neither the Danes nor the Anglo-Saxons won decisive victories, and the eventual outcome of the struggle was the absorption and Christianization of the Danes. There were even a few Danish kings at Winchester and a Danish Archbishop of Canterbury, appointed in 942. The strands of modern Britain were beginning to weave together: the stolid Anglo-Saxons improved agriculture, construction, and industry; the Danes represented all the arts of the sea and trade. In contrast with the brooding traits of the Celtic strain, the Vikings were realists and men of action.

The last successful invasion of the island was undertaken in 1066 by William of Normandy, himself of Viking descent. William was not entirely without claim to the English throne, though he would probably have invaded the country even without so good a pretext. On the hills overlooking the Channel town of Hastings, William fought the forces of Harold for one long day, and by the time night came, the rule of the Wessex kings was over.

The Anglo-Saxons did not take the Normans to their hearts (as Sir Walter Scott reminds us in *Ivanhoe*), but William and his successors set out, with so much vigor and decision, to strengthen and centralize the administration and law of the country that there was no question of their authority. The assimilation of Norman and Anglo-Saxon, though it seems to us now very slow, was inevitable. From William on, the country was practically built anew. The first comprehensive census, *Domesday Book,* taken in 1086, is typical of Norman efficiency. Most of the great cathedrals were begun shortly after the Norman conquest; the great, gray, Norman keeps and castles were built in all parts of the country; and London, a river town which had a life of its own, soon took precedence over Winchester.

The Norman dynasty, however, lasted only three generations and was supplanted by the Plantagenets, beginning with Henry II of Anjou, whose dominions included a large part of western France. The court and nobility spoke French, the people, their own Anglo-Saxon dialects. The English language, combining all its origins, did not take shape until after three more centuries of French rule, centuries which also mark the gradual growth of a national identity.

Henry II, an adept administrator, should be remembered for his instigation of the Common Law, one of Britain's greatest contributions to the world. He also ushered in an era of chivalry, of knights in armor not only playing their parts in jousting tournaments but making the long trek to the Middle East to fight for the new Rome against the Saracens. The Crusades, even though Richard I (the Lionhearted) and Edward I took active part in them, must have

Britain

seemed rather remote to the people of Britain, who were more concerned with building, learning, trading, and creating a united country.

The struggle between the monarchy and the people started early: the date of Magna Carta, symbolizing the uprising of the barons and rich men of London against the oppressions of King John, is 1215. Though the provisions of the document were flouted by many kings after John, the foundation was laid for the development of constitutional monarchy. The long reign which followed, that of Henry III, was marked by a great cultural rebirth, especially the establishment of the Oxford and Cambridge collegiate systems. The revolt of Simon de Montfort and his supporting lords, bishops, citizens, and burgesses against the king's absolute authority began the long struggle for parliamentary government.

The various civil and ecclesiastical reforms, as well as the tremendous improvement of trade and agriculture, of Henry III's reign made it a high-water mark in the country's early history. But by the beginning of the 13th century, largely due to John's rapacious administration, Britain's fortunes had reached a low ebb, and a large part of the French provinces had been lost. It was not until the reign of Edward I (1272–1307), "the English Justinian," that another peak in the graph of British history was reached.

The feudal system, so well constructed by the Normans, was gradually weakened by the kings of the 13th and 14th centuries, who were intent on dominating France. The Hundred Years War, begun by Edward III about 1340 and finished by the spirit of Joan of Arc in 1453, simply cost too much. The British could not put up with the drain forever. They admired the victories of Edward I in subduing Wales and Scotland; they enjoyed Edward III's victories at Crécy and Poitiers; most especially they basked in the glory of Henry V's unlikely achievement at Agincourt, where noble and yeoman fought together; but they didn't like paying, particularly when the tide turned against them, as it frequently did. The growth of Parliament and representative government (the House of Commons emerged in 1339) was directly influenced by the raising of money: the kings who were bent on conquest required Parliament to establish taxes and levies, which were extracted mainly from the developing middle class. The disintegration of feudalism was also hastened by the enormous loss of manpower during the Black Death, which enabled the farm laborer to demand certain rights.

"The Backs" at Cambridge   *Magdalen College, Oxford*

The gardens at Hampton Court Palace

The reign of Henry V (1387–1422) probably stands for the acme of British medieval power and of "Merrie England." By now, England had had her first supreme poet, Geoffrey Chaucer, a cosmopolitan commoner whose work established English as a literary language and probably accelerated its acceptance by the court, Parliament, and schools. The country was united and feeling its power as a nation. In spite of ups and downs, business in the all-important wool trade was good.

For the next sixty years, however, Britain suffered military reverses and internal strife. All the French territories were lost, and the county was devastated by the appalling Wars of the Roses (1455–1485), a title which does no justice to the savage murders and intrigues of a period that has all the flavor of Borgias and Medici.

The conflict over succession, which involved mainly the nobility and left the people out of the slaughter, ended on Bosworth Field in Leicestershire. Richard III, either hero or villain, lay dead, and Henry of Monmouth plucked the crown from a hawthorn bush. The establishment of a Welsh dynasty, the Tudors, began a new surge in Britain's destiny, culminating in the extraordinary Renaissance of the reign of Elizabeth I.

Henry VII, though he was intelligent enough to back the merchant-venturers and encourage the transatlantic explorations of the Italian-born Cabot brothers, foreshadowed the firm absolutism the country could expect under Tudor rule. His son, Henry VIII, in a turbulent reign of thirty-eight years, proved to be a thoroughgoing dictator. Whatever may have been the true causes for his break with the Roman Church, Protestantism in Britain was probably due. Almost two centuries before, John Wycliffe, an Oxford don, had introduced a movement called "Lollardism," which was a curious precursor of the Reformation.

The freeing of Britain from Papal domination was an act of almost foolish bravery in its time, but it was one of the prime factors in the island's eventual national identity. Though there was some see-sawing back and forth for almost another century, the Church of England, with the monarch as its head, was firmly established by Elizabeth I (1533–1603).

Wye Abbey in Herefordshire

It is convenient to call the Elizabethan period the beginning of modern Britain. By turning back the fearsome Spanish Armada in 1588, she became a leading world power, well on the way toward domination of the seas, and internally there was not only tremendous prosperity but also an astonishing flowering of literature and intellect. Shakespeare studies the whole concept of monarchy, penetrates the human conscience, and also gives us a glowing picture of a rowdy, tumultuous society. The grim Norman look of the country gradually changes as the more fanciful Renaissance manor house with its formal flower gardens appears.

Elizabeth was undoubtedly personally popular, but she was hardly less authoritarian than her father. She was only more subtle, more wily, perhaps more hypocritical, than he. The inevitable political conflict did not occur during her reign; with the advent of the Stuarts, a Scottish family less calculated than the robust Tudors to warm the hearts of the increasingly powerful British people, political unrest was apparent. While the basic conflict was a test of power between the King (Charles I), representing absolutism, and Parliament, standing for democratic government, the revolt, when it came, was spearheaded by the Puritans under Oliver Cromwell.

Blood drenched all parts of the land during four years of a desperate civil war that was fought over issues as fundamental as our own Civil War was later. Roundheads against Cavaliers, South against North, middle class against gentry, and, in many cases, brother against brother. On an August day in 1646, at the battle of Preston Pans, the parliamentarian cause prevailed. Charles, an affable and cultivated king who seems only to have misjudged the pattern of his times, was tried, sentenced to death, and beheaded.

For eleven years, during the "Commonwealth," Britain had its first taste of republican rule under Cromwell, styled Lord Protector. But, as so often happens after a successful revolution, the reaction was too violent. Cromwell's Puritan rule could hardly be called lenient. He too had his own quarrels with Parliament, and at the same time had to fight against various uprisings and threats from the Continent. The bitterness caused by the Civil War was not washed away overnight.

Cromwell's death and the subsequent return of Charles II, who re-entered Britain under a canopy of amnesties and reconciliation, came as a great relief to the people. The Revolution, however, had established once and for all the principle of constitutional monarchy, and no event since then has seriously undermined the powers of Parliament. When James II, who followed Charles II, tried to upset the balance and restore Catholic rights, he was summarily deposed, and William of Orange received an invitation to replace him and keep British Protestantism secure. William accepted with haste.

The 17th century, seen as a whole, was a period of extraordinary changes, oscillations between severity and leniency. The Restoration

Medieval stone sculpture at Exeter Cathedral

introduced a new kind of Continental elegance to the worldly court, and brought to the stage the cynical upper-class license of Congreve and Wycherley—a far cry from scholarly John Milton, Cromwell's secretary, who sought to give England its own classical epic. With the swing of the pendulum, great opulence and display, imitating the French court, followed the tight-lipped rigors of Puritanism. People of the town wore fantastic clothes, men took to immense wigs and high-heeled slippers, and ostentatious mansions were built. This show of conspicuous consumption has often, in many countries, been the aftermath of war and repression.

20 Britain

But at the same time, important social and political changes were going on. The formation of the Whigs started the British political-party system on its way. Parliament, stroke by stroke, was defining its own rights and those of the monarchy. The Act of Settlement (1701) set down the terms of modern British government, and the Union of Scotland and England, six years later (at which time the "Union Jack" was adopted), sought to end the unsuccessful attempts of Scottish pretenders to the throne and bring the entire island under the rule of Parliament.

Expansion of trade followed the political stability established at the beginning of the 18th century. A German dynasty, the Hanoverians now ascended the throne. Like the other foreign families who had ruled Britain, they eventually became British by absorption. In spite of wars, the 18th century was one of important advances in industry and commerce. Culturally, it was called the "Augustan age," claiming kinship with the classical periods of Greece and Rome. In an atmosphere of smugness, urbanity, and wit, Pope was writing his elegant couplets; Gibbon was working on his enormous study of the Roman Empire; Robert Burns was creating lilting poetry in Scottish dialect; and Edmund Burke was speaking out on politics. The handsome style of architecture we have come to call "Georgian" changed the face and features of large parts of Britain, and set its indelible mark on such fashionable centers as Bath and Brighton. Robert Adam was decorating Palladian country estates, and Sheraton and Chippendale were building the delicate furniture that is so famous today. James Watt's invention of the steam engine in 1769 was the beginning of the Industrial Revolution. Increased explorations, the eternal search for new trade routes, began to make the entire world smaller and more accessible.

Lichfield: Dr. Johnson's birthplace *The Abbey: Shakespeare Memorial*

Anne Hathaway's cottage at Stratford

The sense of having attained an unsurpassable level of civilization was disturbed by the loss of the American colonies. That was a shock indeed: after a long diet of victories, the British had forgotten the flavor of defeat. But that was simply a blunder which the country must be sure never to repeat. Canada, India, Australia would not be lost the same way.

The French Revolution was another shock to the British, and the subsequent rise of Napoleon threatened not only their world position but the foundations of their society. The British have always seemed to be at their best when sorely pressed, and this was a fight for survival. At Trafalgar, in 1805, Nelson's fleet finally assured Britain of maritime superiority over the French. And ten years later, at the hands of Wellington (with some vital help from European allies), the aspirations of Napoleon were once and for all crushed.

The long years of war with the French had not devastated Britain. This was a war of professionals: all you have to do is compare Thackeray's treatment of Waterloo in *Vanity Fair* with a World War play like Robert Sherriff's *Journey's End,* to see how different the two forms of warfare were. But the Napoleonic Wars had disruptive effects on the whole nation, and were followed by a severe depression, repressive acts by a Tory-dominated cabinet, and the popular unrest which is usually a prologue to great social changes.

The Industrial Revolution had been gathering momentum for some time, much to the horror of such poets as Wordsworth, who begged for a return to the pastoral life. While the Industrial Revolution was defacing large parts of the island with mills and factories and hideous rows of workers' dwellings, it was also leading to vital

Old market town of Shaftesbury in Dorset

reforms. The social structure of Britain was rapidly changing into a greater consciousness of class. The workers became a huge body which, when organized, could press for liberalization of laws, as well as an expanded franchise. Britain had, in fact, become a number of nations: the court and the nobility, the landed gentry, the pushing middle class of factory-owners, the farmers, and the teeming workers.

In 1837 a slip of a girl, eighteen-year-old Victoria, packed her bags and moved from Kensington Palace, where she had lived, to Buckingham Palace, where she became Queen and fixed her name to a period of British history that lasted almost sixty-five years. Her husband's Crystal Palace exhibition in 1851 gave notice to the world that Britain had an empire on which the sun never set and an industrial expansion unmatched by any other country. Britain was providing the world with railroads, cotton goods, coal, and bridges. On the other hand, her arrogant imperialism did not make her popular; envious nations called her "perfidious Albion." She did not mind, secure in the certainty of her own superiority and wealth. The tune was hers to call.

Under the surface of prosperity, industrial conditions at home were badly in need of reform. Humanitarians like Dickens exposed more and more injustices, deprivation, shocking working and living conditions. The government made slow but steady moves toward reform. The Liberal Party brought radical pressures to bear, and a bearded foreigner who had been hard at work in the Reading Room of the British Museum evolved a whole new theory of economics and politics, called "socialism," which indirectly brought into being the Independent Labour Party, founded in 1893.

We have been taught to think of the Victorian era as one of prim propriety—religious, sober and dedicated. What seems closer to the truth is that behind the prim facade there existed a way of life as robust and untrammeled as that of "Merrie England." Britain had a public and a private face—something new in its history.

The Boer War (1899–1902) may signify the point at which British power exceeded itself. There were intense feelings for and against the war itself. Though technically the British won, it was a brittle victory and it was followed by a sense of shame and a certain loss of self-

The Background of Great Britain

confidence. All of Europe was then rustling with unrest, and Germany was developing into a powerful competitor and antagonist of Great Britain. When war came in 1914, the British fought with everything they had, and, though their side won, they were drained and disillusioned by the conflict. Victory had been bought at too dear a price.

After the postwar prosperity, the country was then ravaged by the great depression which followed. These were the years that Robert Graves and Alan Hodge aptly called "The Long Week End." Between 1930 and 1939, Britain made tremendous efforts at recovery, but the era of stupendous international power had passed, and World War II broke out while the country was still weak and unprepared.

Where does Britain go now? She has made an astonishing recovery since World War II, in spite of granting independence to India and losing many of her possessions and markets all over the world. She has been rebuilding, while trying to make a realistic adjustment to things as they are. As far as it is possible in this unstable world, she has achieved stability.

But since about 1900, a great, though quiet, social upheaval has been going on. The class structure shows signs of disintegrating, just as the medieval feudal system finally had to give way to progress. The Labour Party, while in power between 1945–51, introduced the concept of the "Welfare State," and no future government is likely to go back on that. The gap between poor and rich has narrowed to a remarkable degree. A slight Americanization has taken place: the youngsters go for rock-and-roll, drink Coca-Cola, and London has recently even sprouted a number of "hamburger joints." More Britons than ever before can afford to travel on the Continent, and the Lancashire accent can be heard on the Riviera, where it used to be a rare note indeed. The stenographer is saving to have her holidays in Switzerland this year, instead of Blackpool or Brighton.

Britain will always be insular, but she may become less insulated and more adaptable. Her history, far from being one of steady growth, has been more like a business chart's line of peaks and valleys. Her worst periods have always proven to be only turning points, and her current trend cannot yet be assessed.

The Queen's coach at State Opening of Parliament

CHAPTER 3

WHAT YOU SHOULD KNOW ABOUT BRITAIN

PREPARATIONS
Preparing to travel is such a personal matter that any advice must be general. Some people like to have a trip completely mapped out for them in advance; others prefer to "play it by ear." If your time is limited, you'll be better off having some kind of itinerary; but if you can stay several months, you may well want to wait and see what attracts you once you're there. In either case, it's a good idea to have a general notion of where you want to go and what you want to concentrate on: how much time you care to devote to, say, the cathedrals of Britain, or which of the various annual Festivals you may be able to work into your schedule.

If you plan to travel in season (May 15 to September 15), you will definitely have to make arrangements ahead. Hotels, especially in London, are always crowded then, and tickets for the events you might want to see are hard to get. If you travel out of season, your chances of finding hotel accommodations at the last minute are much better.

Your travel agent can help you prepare an itinerary, make your traveling arrangements, reserve hotel accommodations, and even buy tickets for theater and sports events for you. In order to sort out your ideas and get some clues about what Britain has to offer the tourist, make use of Chapters Four through Six in this book. Various brochures are also obtainable from the British Tourist Authority: 680 Fifth Ave., New York, N.Y. 10019; 875 North Michigan Ave., Chicago, Ill. 60611; 612 S. Flower St., Los Angeles, Cal. 90017.

One piece of advice: Don't arrive at Southampton or London Airport with no idea in the world of how you want to spend the time at your disposal. Your time will be wasted.

In Britain, you are never far from a pub

26 Britain

Costs. Many travelers like to (or have to) budget their trips, and here, too, only general advice is possible. You can pay for most of your trip even before you arrive in Great Britain, arranging to do so through your travel agent. There's a drawback, though. You'll be committed to a rigid itinerary, with very little leeway for the unexpected. A better idea is to pay in advance for large expenses, such as hotel rooms and railroad trips, but to leave the incidentals to be paid for in Britain. There's nothing wrong, of course, with paying as you go.

It is possible to live and travel comfortably in Britain for as little as $12 to $16 a day. It can even be done for $8 a day—or, of course, much more expensively. Almost everything will be cheaper than it is in the U.S., particularly if you are traveling out of season.

Best Time to Travel. In terms of weather, May and September are the months to aim for. British weather is infamous. It's not really *bad* weather, though; it's just unreliable. The rain is not so heavy as it is frequent. The British carry umbrellas and raincoats even on apparently clear days, not because they are eccentric, but because they know how easily a sunny morning can give way to a drizzly afternoon. If there is to be good weather, May and September are the months when it will usually prevail.

The winters are not severe, except in the north and in Scotland, but they *are* damp. And since the British haven't really come to grips with central heating, for most Americans the British winter is a time of misery. If you go in winter be prepared with sweaters and woolen socks and flannel pajamas.

Passport and Medical Requirements are minimal. All an American citizen needs in order to enter Britain is a valid passport, which he gets by applying in person to the U.S. Passport Agency offices in New York, Chicago, Boston, Washington, D.C., San Francisco, New Orleans, Seattle, Philadelphia, Miami, or Honolulu. (If you aren't near any of these cities, your local courthouse will have passport facilities.) You'll need proof of citizenship, birth certificate, two recent photographs 2½ inches square, taken full-face in black and white or color, and finally a ten-dollar bill. It takes up to three weeks between the time you apply and the day your brand-new passport is in your hands. Sometimes it takes longer, so apply as early as possible.

Vaccination is no longer required for re-entry into the United States from Britain and other European countries.

GETTING TO BRITAIN

You have a wide choice, of course, of sea and air transportation. Be sure to reserve well in advance, especially if you're traveling in

What You Should Know About Britain 27

season. Six months ahead is none too early to make plane reservations, and if you are going by ship and want any kind of choice in cabin accommodations, it's best to reserve up to nine months ahead if possible. On ships of the United States, Cunard, French, Holland-American Lines, and various others, the average one-way tourist class fare (in season) starts at about $350; first-class starts at about $600. The least expensive accommodations are usually the earliest to be filled, and you may have to count on paying fares higher than the average.

Special tip: If you plan to travel by ship tourist class, try for one of the all-tourist-class ships, such as the Holland-American *Statendam* or the Greek Lines *Olympia*. You will have better accommodations and the run of the ship.

Airlines offer jet services at varying round-trip prices, from about $280. Airline packages and charter flights run even lower.

British Customs Regulations. If you are entering Britain as a tourist, remaining for a specific period, most of your luggage will be passed through duty-free as personal effects. Gifts of small value, to a total of £10 other than "spirits" (whiskey or gin) or tobacco, are allowed. Tourists are permitted to take in one pound of tobacco in any form (400 cigarettes, for example); one quart bottle of wine and one of spirits; ½ pint of perfume or toilet water; and a reasonable quantity of unexposed film. You will find most British customs officials extremely polite and reasonable. They should be treated with respect for their intelligence and perception.

Leave your pets at home. Animals are allowed into Britain only after spending six months in quarantine, at *your* expense.

Clothes. If you are traveling by plane, you are allowed to carry 66 pounds in first class or 44 pounds in tourist-economy class. In either case you are restricted, and this may be a good thing, since most travelers tend to take too many of their belongings anyway. Don't try to be prepared for all emergencies. There is no necessity you can't buy in Britain.

You will rarely need the extremes of clothing in Britain—neither extra heavy nor extra light clothes. No Bermuda shorts, for example. For a spring or summer trip, you will most likely need a light topcoat; in winter, a heavier overcoat. A lightweight woolen suit (men or women) will have its uses, even in summer, as will a couple of sweaters. Walking shoes are a must. For evening, a man should carry a plain dark suit (unless he plans to be dressy, in which case a dinner jacket will be in order), and a woman, one or two cocktail dresses. (There is less dressing up for the theater than there used to be.) A raincoat and some sort of rain hat will see lots of use.

Many travelers to Britain carry unfilled suitcases, with the intention of buying (at favorable prices) raincoats, sweaters, and men's or women's woolen suits during their visits.

28 Britain

MONEY AND EXCHANGE

For centuries the British currency system, ignoring the decimal system in use throughout the major part of the world, mystified foreign visitors with its shillings, florins, half crowns, pounds and guineas. As of February, 1971, however, the British finally adopted a decimal system of their own. The pound, written £, is still in use, but instead of being made up of twenty shillings, it is now made up of one hundred new pence, written p.

Coins are minted in the following denominations:

½p.	called a half new penny	worth	1.2¢
1p.	" one " "	"	2.5¢
2.p.	" two new pence	"	4.9¢
5p.	" five " "	"	12.3¢
10p.	" ten " "	"	24.5¢
50p.	" fifty " "	"	$1.23

There are bills in the following denominations:
£1	$2.45
£5	$12.25
£10	$24.50
£20	$49.00

One pound plus seventy-five new pence would be written as follows: £1.75, and in American dollars it would be worth $4.29.

Before your departure for Britain, check to see if there is any change in the value of the dollar, as rates of equivalency do change. In recent years, unfortunately, the value of the dollar has been decreasing.

Southampton Docks, perhaps your first stop in England

What You Should Know About Britain 29

In slang, a pound is often called a "quid"; a shilling is called a "bob."

Tailors, doctors, lawyers often express their fees in *guineas*. A guinea used to mean one pound and one shilling is now equivalent to about $1.05.

In general, you are on the right track if you think of a pound as worth about $2.50 and 50 pence as about $1.25. A 10 penny piece has roughly the equivalence of a quarter in the United States.

The British still *talk* in their old currency system, so simply remember that one shilling is really 5 new pence, two shillings 10 p., and 21 shillings is one pound and 5 pence, etc.

The following chart should be of help in translating prices from British to American currency.

1.00	$2.45	3.00	$7.35
1.25	$3.06	4.00	$9.80
1.50	$3.67	5.00	$12.25
1.75	$4.28	6.00	$14.70
2.00	$4.90	7.00	$17.15

The safest way to carry money is, of course, in one form or other of Travelers Checks, which can be bought from the American Express Co. or other banking establishments. They are easily cashed in Britain. At most ports of entry there are *bureaux de change* where you can cash a Travelers Check for your preliminary expenses.

Depending on the international money market, it is sometimes possible to buy pounds sterling for dollars a little more cheaply in the U.S. than in Britain. The difference is so slight, however, that it's probably not a very good idea, since you run the usual risk of theft or loss.

Tipping. Tipping standards are slightly lower in Britain than in the United States. As elsewhere, the tip depends on the type and extent of service you have received. Without trying to work out careful percentages, you can calculate 15 new pence to a pound. For a bill around 50 new pence, the tip can be 5-8 new pence. Where you would be inclined to tip a quarter in the U.S., use a ten pence coin. This applies, for example, to the bellboy delivering something to your hotel room, or to the doorman for getting you a cab.

In some hotels, a service charge of 10 to 15 per cent will be added to your bill. Even so, you might want to give something extra to the porter who carries your bags to your rooms, particularly in a first-class or de luxe establishment. If your hotel bill carries no service charge, then you should distribute 10 to 15 per cent of the bill to the chambermaid, bellboys, hall porter and doorman, in proportion to

Britain

what they have done for you and the length of your stay. For a one-night stay, 10p. is the proper amount for the chambermaid, 15p. for a stay of two days, and 50p. if you have stayed a week.

In fancy West End of London hotels and restaurants you should tip slightly more than elsewhere in the country.

The tip for taxi drivers should never be less than 5 p. If the meter registers anywhere from 25 to 40 pence, a tip of 7p. is appropriate. There need be no embarrassment in asking a taxi driver to give you small change, or even to discuss with him the amount you want him to have. British taxi drivers are used to having foreign visitors hold out a handful of coins and say, "take the right amount."

At airports and railroad stations, porters should be tipped a minimum of 10p. You should tip a little more if he carries your bags a long distance or has to wait while you take care of something else.

For checking your hat and coat, a tip of 5p. is usually enough, a bit more if you are feeling particularly generous. In barber shops 10p. is minimum, in beauty parlors 20p., depending upon the amount of your bill.

In the theater, ushers are not tipped, unless they bring your refreshments during the intermission. You do, however, pay for the program. You do not generally tip the barman or barmaid in pubs. In tearooms, 10% of your bill is sufficient.

GETTING AROUND IN BRITAIN

Because the whole island is so small, traveling in Britain is pleasantly simple. Within a 50-mile radius of London, you are in touch with Oxford, the Thames valley, Windsor, Eton, Cambridge, Canterbury. Extend the radius to 100 miles, and you have reached Stratford-on-Avon, the Cotswolds, Bath, Salisbury, East Anglia, Dorset. The most northerly inhabited place in Scotland, John O'Groats, is just over 700 miles from London. In other words, almost no distance from

English village: church, cottage, farm, and a signpost

What You Should Know About Britain 31

London to anywhere on the island is nearly as great as that between New York and Chicago.

Railroads. The British Railways, the nationalized railroad system, provide services to almost everywhere on the island. There are two classes, first and second, as well as Pullmans (like American parlor cars) and sleeping cars on long-distance runs. There are special railroad rates available for the tourist if arrangements and payment are made ahead in the U.S. British Rail offices in North America sell Thrift Coupon books which allow a reduction in fares. There is also a British-Rail-Pass scheme, which allows unlimited travel in Britain for from 8 days ($30) to a month ($80). There are also a surprising number of one-day excursions and special low-rate trips available within Britain itself. Tickets for all journeys can be bought through American Express, or at any of the many British Rail or Cook's offices in central London. Don't forget to make sure which station your train is leaving from—London has a multitude of stations.

Air Travel is highly developed in Britain, offering connections between London and Birmingham, Manchester, Liverpool, Edinburgh, Glasgow, Aberdeen. Air services are also the most convenient means of reaching the Channel Islands and, in the north, the Shetlands, Orkneys, and Hebrides.

Buses offer an inexpensive way to tour the country. Many travelers prefer them to trains and planes, feeling that they see more of the countryside this way. Long-distance buses are called "express coaches"; many of these lines offer set tours with stopovers.

Automobile. At the height of the season, it is advisable to arrange for car-hire well ahead of your arrival. This can be done in the U.S., through Hertz International; or your travel agent can take care of it for you. In season, a self-drive car can be hired for about $45 a week plus 8¢ a mile; out of season the charge is slightly less. You pay for the gas at about 75¢ an Imperial gallon (1.2 U.S. gallons).

A valid American driver's license is accepted in Britain. The only driving problem the American visitor faces is keeping to the left side of the road. Don't go out on the road alone the first time; have someone along to keep saying "Left." Driving conditions, in general, are good, though most roads are narrower than Americans are used to. Parts of Devon and Cornwall specialize in treacherous roads, hanging on clifftops, and full of hairpin bends. Just slow down there and you'll be all right. Driving manners are a cut above those you'll find anywhere else in the world. But beware of the car with the red *L* for "Learner" displayed on the back bumper. He hasn't passed his driver's test—and maybe for good reason. Gasoline (petrol) is more expensive in Britain than it is in the U.S., but most British cars use much less gas per mile, so it works out about even. Inquiries should be made through the American Automobile Association, 1712 G Street, N. W., Washington, D.C. 20006.

32 Britain

Getting Around in London. Although London is a big and sprawling city, getting around in it is extraordinarily easy and agreeable.

The *subways,* called "the underground" or "the tube," cover most of Greater London. The fare depends on the distance traveled, the average (unless you're heading for the suburbs) being between 12¢ and 37¢. Smoking is allowed, and well-placed maps indicate with commendable clarity exactly where every station is.

The famous London *buses* are bright red double-deckers. Again, the fare depends on the distance, and smoking is allowed on the upper deck.

In addition, London transport provides the services of Green Line buses, single-deckers, which operate between London and suburban areas, as far afield as Windsor and Guildford and parts of Kent.

If you are in any doubt about how to get from one place to another in the city, just telephone 222 1234, and an operator will tell you the easiest route.

American travelers usually find London *taxis* an ideal form of travel in the city. The taxis are small and agile; they can turn on a sixpence. The driver expects you to keep the glass panel between his section and yours closed for privacy. Until recently, they were also extremely cheap; they are even now somewhat cheaper than taxis in the U.S.

A London taxi driver has an illuminated sign on the front of his car to show that he is free. There are a number of taxi ranks all over London, where you can telephone for a taxi to come to your door. (These phones are listed in the phone book under "Taxicab.")

Outside of London, taxis are usually found at railroad stations. Otherwise they have to be ordered by telephone.

HOTELS

As stated before, it is always a good idea, if possible, to reserve hotel accommodations in Britain beforehand. Considering the number of tourists who arrive in the country annually, there is an acute shortage of space.

Though British hotels generally offer good accommodations and service, they are wildly variable. The luxury hotels, of course, are as good as those anywhere in the world. But outside of London, and in the moderate-price class, British hotels often have no central heating, few private baths, and faded décor. Fortunately there are many exceptions—hotels of great charm and atmosphere with prices much lower than the American equivalent. They will be listed in later pages.

You can be sure of central heating only in the de luxe and first-class hotels in the large cities. Almost always, however, rooms will be provided with gas or electric heaters, and in the country, hot water bottles are usually provided when the temperature is low.

Private baths are increasingly available, but if you choose a room

The Local, an English institution

without one, you will find that most establishments have enough bathrooms, and they are usually clean and well kept. Almost all rooms have hot and cold running water.

Cleaning and laundry service will be provided in most British hotels. London has many first-class establishments; elsewhere in the country, the level of cleaning will probably be disappointing to the American traveler. Both services are relatively expensive in Britain.

In the country, where hotels are few and far between, you are better off staying in an inn. The atmosphere is likely to be a lot cozier, and an old-fashioned sense of comfort still exists off the beaten track.

Prices quoted in Chapter Seven for most British hotels include bed and breakfast. In London, this tradition is beginning to die out, but not in the provinces and in the country.

Try not to get stuck in Britain without accommodation, but if you are, the following two addresses may be of help:

LONDON TOURIST BOARD, 4 Grosvenor Gardens, S.W. 1 (730-9845).
HOTEL ACCOMMODATION SERVICE from 7:30 A.M. to 11 A.M.
HOTAC, 93 Baker St., W. 1 (730-0791)

PUBS AND INNS

"Pubs" are public houses (usually owned by a particular brewery, but sometimes a so-called "free house" selling several brands) offering drink but no accommodations. Inns, generally of an earlier vintage, offer both. Inns and pubs are something more than just drinking places; they also serve a useful social function. Most city dwellers have their "locals," where they go regularly to meet their friends, play darts, and discuss the state of the country. Country pubs are used in the same way. They are good places in which to study the British character.

British beer is famous, quite different from American beer, and a matter of personal taste. Draught beer: "mild" (dark-colored) or "bitter" (light-colored) or a combination of both are the most popular. Not iced, and rather lifeless compared with what we are used to, it is worth trying all the same. It's really not as different (or as bad) as it has been cracked up to be. If you prefer to stick to something more familiar, the nearest approximation is either bottled light ale or lager which *is* often iced. The bottled product costs about 10p., while a half-pint of bitter or mild is about 8p.

Pubs and inns also sell sherry and "spirits" (whisky or gin). Whisky, to the Briton, simply means Scotch. If you want Irish, Canadian Club, bourbon or rye and if it is available, you have to specify. "A whisky" is a small measure and will come to you in an extremely small glass. If you want a bigger drink, you'll have to ask for, and pay for, a double. (Price is usually 20p., double 50p. More, of course, in fashionable hotel cocktail lounges.)

A favorite drink in any pub is cider, because it is cheap (about 5p. a pint) and, being *hard* cider, has a quick action.

Mixed drinks are rarely available in pubs and inns. If you're longing for a Martini, whiskey sour, or the like, you'll have to take your chances in a hotel. In London, at the Connaught, the Ritz, the Mayfair, or any of the similar hotels, you will get excellent drinks of all kinds, and you'll pay about $1.25 for them.

As almost everyone knows, pubs are generally divided into two parts: the Public Bar and the Saloon Bar (or Lounge). This is one of the most obvious continuing symbols of British class distinction: the customers in the Public are usually working people and the beer is a penny or two cheaper there. It is not a serious *gaffe* for the uninformed American visitor to wander into the Public Bar; indeed, he may choose to stay there. But as a rule, he is expected to use the Saloon Bar. It's one of those tacit arrangements.

Eating and Drinking Hours. Being an orderly people, the British expect you to eat at a decent hour. The Italians and Spanish may be content to start their leisurely dinners around ten in the evening, but by then, most Britons will be thinking of going to bed. As a result it may be difficult to dine inexpensively late at night. In London a number of high-class restaurants stay open (for a full dinner you want to get there by 10:30) as do most Indian, Chinese, and even Italian and Greek restaurants. Elsewhere, because of the catering laws many hotel dining rooms close at 10:30, and by midnight you have to be extremely appealing to get even a thin sandwich. Otherwise you'll have to rely on all-night tea stalls (far from appetizing) that service taxi and truck drivers, or on the growing number of espresso houses which offer snacks as well as coffee. In the larger provincial cities

What You Should Know About Britain 35

you'll find a few expensive establishments open late and sometimes a coffee house.

Your drinking habits will be even more severely regulated. The licensing laws, which came into being toward the end of World War I and have continued in existence for obscure reasons, govern the operating hours of all cocktail lounges, pubs, inns and liquor shops. Restaurants, too, can sell alcohol only at these hours. The drinking period is generally from 11:30 A.M. to 3 P.M., and again from 5 P.M. to 10:30 or 11 P.M., the hours varying slightly in different localities. You will become quite accustomed to the closing calls: "Time, please!" "Drink up now!" "Your glasses, please, gentlemen!" (In pubs, clocks are always set ten minutes ahead, so that uncooperative patrons can be dealt with before the doors must actually be locked.) Some hotels, restaurants, and night clubs (often "private" clubs) are specially licensed to serve drinks at later hours. The law is strictly enforced, and neither begging nor bribing will do you any good, unless you hit a rare pocket of corruption.

If you want to keep a drink handy in your hotel room, don't buy a bottle from room service; it will be half the price in a liquor shop.

FOOD AND WINE

Visitors make too much fuss about British food. Like the weather, it is extremely variable and undependable. You can go to a fancy, expensive restaurant in London and have an abominable meal; you can wander into an inn you never heard of out in the country, and have a delicious three-course dinner at very little cost. It's often a matter of luck, but check at the back of this book for generally reliable restaurants. Don't expect a gourmet's paradise.

To be specific: *Fish* is usually excellent in Britain, fresh and nicely cooked. Try skate, bream, turbot, plaice, and halibut. Dover sole is a national specialty, and can be ordered with a variety of about thirty sauces. Salmon in season is a treat, and British smoked salmon, in any season, is tops. Fish and chips is a safe dish in inexpensive restaurants, particularly if the fish used is plaice. (Steer clear of the

A brushmaker's sign in Westmorland

fish-and-chips café, where you are given a fatty mess of some unnamed fish in a cone of newspaper.) *Sea food* is also good and safe to order, but keep away from streetside venders of "cockles and winkles." Oysters are eaten with only lemon juice or vinegar and red pepper—no tomato sauce.

Try *kippers* (small smoked herrings) and *finnan haddie* (smoked haddock); they are specialties and good if you like them.

The British do know how to *roast beef, lamb, and pork*. Order these rather than anything that requires a fancy sauce. *Roast chicken* and *duck,* as well as *game,* are likely to be successful.

Here are some specialties you ought to try:

Steak and kidney pie—cubes of high-quality beef steak and veal or lamb kidneys, baked under a crust which only the British seem able to make.

Yorkshire pudding—the natural accompaniment to roast beef, a flour-and-egg batter baked in beef drippings until it is crisp outside and soft inside.

Veal and ham pie—a cold dish, slices of meat in jelly, baked in a pastry.

Cornish pasty—a turnover with chopped meat in it.

Baked potatoes—not what you expect, but peeled potatoes roasted in beef drippings.

Hors d'oeuvres—usually a nice selection of fish and marinated salads.

Boiled gammon—a part of the pork Americans usually use for bacon, lean very tasty.

British *cheeses* are largely undiscovered by Americans, and they are very good indeed. Apart from the well-known Cheddar, there are Stilton (a subtle "blue" cheese), Cheshire (both white and pink), Gloucester, Caerphilly, Wensleydale, and many others found locally throughout the country. They are milder than many of the famous Continental cheeses, but distinctive and first-rate.

Where the British fall down badly is in their vegetables and desserts. Overcooked cabbage or Brussels sprouts and potatoes are practically universal, and can easily ruin a beautifully rare slice of roast sirloin of beef. This cannot be helped, and one simply has to put up with it. In restaurants with a Continental cuisine, the vegetables are often better cooked, though not always. Try to order salads whenever possible, or grilled tomatoes—anything that is not boiled.

Desserts (called "sweets") are indescribable to those who have never experienced them. One handy rule is to say "no custard" when ordering a dessert in any but the top restaurants; for a rather distasteful synthetic egg custard is ladled on practically everything to achieve—it seems—uniformity of appearance. Fruit tarts are sometimes good, and mincemeat pie in cold weather is palatable. "Trifle" (a

What You Should Know About Britain 37

curious combination of old cake, jello and sherry) and suet puddings are best avoided. If you see fresh fruit on the menu, order it in preference to all prepared desserts. The *savory,* as an after-dinner course, is not often attractive to the American taste. Consisting as it does of mushrooms on toast, or kidney on toast, or sardines, it is easy to turn down.

No kind word can be said for the coffee, except in the many expresso bars that have popped up in the big cities. Either go to one of these for coffee after your meal, or else order tea.

You will be surprised by the excellence and abundance of hotel breakfasts. You will have a choice of fruit juices or stewed fruit, cooked cereals, eggs and bacon, fish, cold toast, and questionable coffee or safe tea.

Though a few hardy souls in the country make an effort to produce wine for their own consumption, there are no British wines. The choice of French wines, however, is tremendous, and the prices aren't high by our standards. Bordeaux reds are called "clarets," and German Rhine wines, "hock." There are also fair South African wines, which cost much less; and a surprising array of wines from Yugoslavia, Hungary, Spain and other less familiar places. None of these approach the French wines, but you may care to experiment with them.

ENTERTAINMENT

Theater. For many visitors, the theater is one of Britain's primary attractions. While there are, naturally, both good and rather poor productions, the general level is extremely high. One of the visitor's advantages is that the theater season runs straight through the year. In fact, new productions are mounted in great numbers during the months of May and June, to coincide with the beginning of the London social "season."

You'll be pleased to find that tickets to most shows are not difficult to get, even at the last minute. A "hit" in London does not necessarily mean a show sold out months in advance, but one which sells out each night. Tickets are much cheaper than they are in New

Local playhouse—good entertainment isn't limited to London

York, though prices have gradually been creeping up. £1.50 ($3.60) is generally the price for best orchestra seats (called "stalls"). At the other extreme, most theaters have unreserved seats in the gallery for as little as $1, though these can only be bought on the day of the performance. Smoking is not permitted in most theaters. Coffee or tea can sometimes be ordered at your seat during intermissions, and don't be surprised to find your British neighbors eating chocolates during the show. There are bars in all British theaters. Your program will cost 5p.–15p.

Theater tickets can be bought either at the individual box offices, at American Express, at some hotels and department stores, or at ticket agencies, which abound in central London. The extra charge for a ticket bought from an agency is generally 12p. (30¢). One of the curious aspects of buying theater seats in London is that people tend to order tickets for a particular theater rather than a particular play. "Two stalls for July 2 at Drury Lane," is what you hear more often than "Two stalls for *My Fair Lady*."

During the war, curtain time was brought forward to 6 P.M. Ever since, there has been a slow move back to the original opening hour, but most theaters today begin at 7:30 or 8 P.M. In recent years, many shows (particularly musicals) have started the habit of a late matinee at 5:30 or 6 P.M., with the evening performance that day at 8 or 8:30.

Most Americans will be thoroughly familiar with the kind of plays produced in Britain. Only one warning is necessary: Beware of the English *farce* and the Christmas *pantomime*. Both are British to the bone, and nine times out of ten the visiting American, unless he has a scholarly interest in such matters, will not care for them.

Though London is the center of theatrical activity in Britain, there are very good theaters in other parts of the country. Many plays have tryout runs in such cities as Brighton, Manchester, Newcastle and Edinburgh. There are excellent repertory companies in various cities, including Bristol, Coventry, Birmingham, Oxford, Cambridge, etc. The season of Shakespeare repertory given annually at Stratford-on-Avon (April to November) is one of the most popular lures for tourists; seats must be reserved well ahead. The Edinburgh Festival in August also includes several interesting theatrical events.

Music and Ballet. London supports two opera houses during the autumn and winter seasons: Covent Garden and Sadlers Wells. Ballet performances are also given in both houses; and a third ballet company, the London Festival Ballet, has several seasons during the year at the new Royal Festival Hall, on the South Bank.

There are at least four first-class symphony orchestras in London which provide well-balanced concerts with important soloists. A summer feature is the popular Promenade Concerts (called "The

Proms") at Albert Hall. Orchestras in Manchester, Edinburgh and Bournemouth are also highly regarded. During the spring and summer, there are a number of most interesting musical festivals in Britain. The Glyndebourne Opera Festival (May-August) takes place in a setting of amazing beauty and luxury: a private country estate in Sussex. The Aldeburgh Festival, run by Benjamin Britten, in a charming town on the East Anglia coast, takes place in June. The Cheltenham Festival of Contemporary Music is usually scheduled in July, and attracts all those who are interested in the musical *avant garde*. The Edinburgh Festival naturally features among its arrangements music by the great orchestras, ensembles, and soloists of the world, as does the Bath Festival, in May or June.

SPORTS

Soccer. The tourist in Britain has a wide variety of sports (spectator or participating) to choose from. The sport claiming the highest popular attendance in the country is Association football (professional soccer): the season is from mid-August to early May. Though a newspaper like the *Times* pays little attention to "Association," the other papers are full of it, giving details of player tradings, the fantastic salaries offered one star or another, and trying to predict the outcome of all matches. The Cup Final, played at Wembley in May, causes a World Series atmosphere, and London, on the night before and after the game, is full of supporters, up from the provinces, who bring an air of cheerful rowdiness to the capital.

Rugby. Nonprofessional rugby (more like American football) is played from late September to mid-April, and has an enthusiastic following. The greatest excitement is reserved for the International Matches, between England and Wales, or Wales and Scotland. When the Rugby Final is played at Twickenham, boisterous fans, who go in for nationalistic "larks," can turn the fountains at Trafalgar Square into a scene of virtual riot, depending on the outcome of the match.

Cricket. The American football fan may find both Association and rugby rather tame, and he will miss the collegiate atmosphere of our own football season. But what is the American baseball fan to make of cricket, the British summer game? Besides having a language all its own, with expressions like "hat-trick," "century," "bowled out," "caught off leg," etc., its pace compares with that of baseball as a bicycle compares with a Boeing-707. Though he may suffer with boredom, the American sports lover ought to attend at least one match at Lord's Cricket Grounds or the Oval in London. You can always wander off to the pavilion for refreshment when you've lost

Riding to the hounds—the Croome Hunt, Worcestershire

track. Village cricket is in some ways more interesting, for it involves small communities and is more intimate.

Racing. Horse racing is probably the most rewarding of British spectator sports, from the American point of view. The flat-racing season goes from the end of March to the end of November. Hurdle, or steeplechase, racing takes up the winter months, leading to its climax in the Grand National Steeplechase at Liverpool in March. The main events of the flat-racing season are the Cambridgeshire, the Derby, the Cesarewitch, the Royal Ascot season, and the Goodwood Stakes. Britons of all classes take their racing very seriously, and the major events often have the air of a great carnival.

Greyhound racing is a popular sport with the working classes; London has several tracks, and the betting is furious.

Golf. For the visiting sportsman who feels the urge to exercise his own muscles rather than watch professionals or amateurs exercising theirs, golf is probably the most attractive of British sports. There is no shortage of courses and clubs throughout the country, and Americans are made welcome at practically all of them. The sensible approach, unless you have a personal introduction, is to telephone the secretary of the club where you would like to play. In the London area, there are public courses at Richmond Park, Chingford, Mitcham Common and Addington (near Croydon). Outside of London, the best-known courses are Wentworth, Sunningdale and Royal Mid-Surrey. The Scottish courses at St. Andrews and Gleneagles are world famous. Others of equal quality are located at Sandwich and Deal (in Kent) and Hoylake (near Liverpool). A charming course well worth a visit is at the beach resort of Westward Ho! in Devon.

Fishing. Britain is a fisherman's delight. From April to October, trout and salmon are abundant in Scotland, Wales, Yorkshire and southern England. You can charter fishing boats off the South Coast for excellent deep-sea fishing: the major catch is *tope*, which come as heavy as forty pounds. Game fishing (trout and salmon) is particularly challenging in the many streams of Devon and Cornwall. You have to stay at a hotel owning fishing rights, or else buy fishing tickets from the owner of the banks where you wish to try your luck. Both the Severn and Wye Rivers are famous for the salmon, and deep-sea fishing is plentiful all along the north and west coasts of Wales.

What You Should Know About Britain

"Coarse fishing" (the British expression for all but game fishing) is excellent in the East Anglian Broad, where roach and bream are abundant. For lake trout, perch, pike and eel (both rod and net fishing) you will want to visit the Lake District in northern England. Be sure to make local inquiries before you get your rod all set: some fishing areas are privately owned, and in others a fee is required.

HISTORIC HOMES AND GARDENS

Over the centuries, the British (with means) have built castles, manor houses, country estates, of which over 400 are now periodically open to the public. These are not only examples of great architectural skill and taste, amazing splendor and beauty, but many have the extra charm of still being lived in—often by descendants of the family that originally built them. The present Duke of Marlborough, for example, still lives at Blenheim Palace, and sometimes appears from his private apartments to have a word with visitors being shown around his home. The greatest periods of building were the 17th and 18th centuries, but some of the well-known castles go back to Norman and Elizabethan times. Houses like Haddon Hall, Hatfield House, Burghley House, not to mention the royal palaces such as Hampton Court and Kensington Palace, are full of historical interest and great works of art.

Don't start off on a tour of these homes without a copy of *Historic Houses and Castles in Great Britain and Northern Ireland,* published by ABC Travel Guides, available at most bookshops and from the British Tourist Authority. Each of the houses open to the public is listed and described in this publication, with the days and hours when entry is permitted.

The famous and superb British gardens, such as those at Hampton Court, Warwick Castle, Stourhead Park, and many others, should not be neglected.

The guides provided at these homes are usually extremely well-informed men and women who will fill you in on all you want to know. The general fee for a visit is $17\frac{1}{2}$p. Though a tip to the guides is not required, they rarely refuse 10p. as they say good-bye to you at the front door.

Burghley House in Northamptonshire

Britain

SHOPPING

London is, of course, one of the leading shopping centers of the world, providing as it does a number of comprehensive department stores, as well as specialty shops of all kinds.

General Shopping. The leading department stores in London are Harrods, Selfridge's, Liberty's, and the Army and Navy Stores. These provide everything, from pins to pillows, frames to Frigidaires. A very special kind of department store is Fortnum and Mason, in Piccadilly, where you are likely to run into titled ladies or famous actors buying expensive fruits and vegetables, canned goods, wines, perfumes, Dior clothes, Christmas cards or woolen sweaters.

Clothes. For men's ready-made clothes, the best medium-priced shops are Gieve's (Bond Street), Simpsons (Piccadilly), Aquascutum (Regent Street) and Jaeger's (Regent Street). The best selection of sweaters is found at Liberty's, various shops along Burlington Arcade, Jaeger's, and Hector Powe (Regent Street). Shops specializing in women's ready-made clothes are Dickins and Jones; Harvey, Nichols & Co.; Marshall and Snelgrove. Most of the above-mentioned shops have a pretty good selection of men's jackets and coats, and women's suits. If you have time to have clothes made, Savile Row, of course, is famous—but not cheap. Blades (8 Burlington Gardens) tailors women's as well as men's suits. A traditionally fine men's hat shop is Herbert Johnson (New Bond Street); more famous is Scott's, at the corner of Bond St. and Piccadilly. The best shoeshops, both custom- and ready-made, are all in Mayfair. But if your tastes are more "mod," and you tend to like your clothes to flash like neon signs, you should visit Carnaby Street, on the decidedly less conservative side of Regent Street, on the edge of Soho. The clothes are cheap, and though not of the best quality, they *do* swing.

Antiques. Britain is a mine of antique furniture, much of it to be found (expensively) in London West End shops, as well as (more cheaply) in places like Brighton and Windsor, and all the out-of-the-way shops you will come upon as you travel through the country. The antique hunter may also want to haunt the old-established auction rooms of Christie's, 8 King St., St. James's, S.W.1. (839-9060), and Sotheby's at 34 New Bond St., S.W.1 (493-7242).

Those interested in antique silver of all kinds should not fail to visit the "silver vaults" at the Chancery Lane Safe Deposit and Offices Co., Ltd., 65 Chancery Lane, W.C.2. Nowhere else in the world will you see such an extraordinary collection of old Sheffield and sterling pieces, at prices which are fairly reasonable.

Street Markets. For a different kind of view of London, the tourist might look in on the street markets of Berwick Street (weekdays),

What You Should Know About Britain 43

Petticoat Lane (Sundays) and the Portobello Road (Saturdays), places where food is sold on pushcarts, along with junk and an occasional object of value.

GETTING ON IN BRITAIN—FACTS AND ADVICE

Electric Current. Think twice about carrying electrical equipment to Britain. The British system is mostly 220 to 250 volts A.C., 50 cycles, and American appliances are generally geared to 120 volts and 60 cycles. What is more, the British have a most peculiar system of electrical outlets—at least three different varieties, none of which coincide with American plugs. Many city hotels, however, do provide appropriate wired outlets for American electric shavers.

Legal Holidays. In England and Wales, six legal holidays (called "bank holidays") are observed: Good Friday, Easter Monday, a late-spring Monday, the last Monday in August ("August Bank Holiday"), Christmas, and Boxing Day (December 26). In Scotland the legal holidays are New Year's Day, Good Friday, first Monday in May, first Monday in August, Christmas Day.

On most of the legal holidays, and especially on Christmas and Boxing Days, London and the other large cities close up tight, and it is almost impossible to find a place to have a meal.

Business Hours. The usual business and shopping hours throughout Britain are from 9 A.M. to 5:30 P.M., without a lunchtime interruption. Banks are open from 9:30 A.M. to 3:30 P.M. daily, closed on Saturdays. Most shops and retail houses have half-day closing one day a week, but most department stores now remain open all day Saturday.

Postal, Telephone and Telegraph Services are all combined under the postal system.

Postal rates from Britain are as follows:
To Europe (all goes by air)—letters 5p., postcards 3p.
To U.S. (surface)—letters 5p., postcards 3p.
(air)—letters, 8p., postcards 5p.
(One-sheet air letters may also be bought at the bargain price of 5p.
Local letters and postcards—first class 3p., second class $2\frac{1}{2}$p.

Telegrams sent within Britain and to the Continent can be sent from any post office or by phone (dial 190). The internal rate 25p. for 12 words, 2p. for each additional word. Overnight telegrams can be sent at the rate of $12\frac{1}{2}$p. for 12 words.

Cablegrams to the U.S. and Canada can be sent by phone (call 557) or at the Western Union, post office, or Commercial Cable & Wireless.

44 Britain

Most post offices are open daily from 9 A.M. to 5:30 P.M. In London, the Trafalgar Square branch is open at all times (located at St. Martin's Place, W.C.2, 930-9580).

Public telephones are found in post offices, railroad stations and street kiosks—*not* in restaurants, chemist shops or newspaper shops. All public telephones cost 2p. for a local call. There are instructions in every call-box. Read them carefully. You can dial 100 for the operator without inserting any money, and in emergencies you can also dial 999 free.

To make a long-distance call from London you dial 100 (the operator). Many internal long-distance calls can be dialled directly from the call-box and paid for as they happen.

If you are going to phone to the U.S. it is best to reserve a special hour ahead, so that the circuits will be free and the operator can make sure that your party will be at the other end.

SOME USEFUL ADDRESSES

American Automobile Association, 15 Pall Mall, London, S.W.1.

American Express:
  LONDON—   Haymarket, S.W.1.
  LIVERPOOL—   India Bldgs., Water St.
  SOUTHAMPTON—Havelock Chambers, Queens Terrace.
  EDINBURGH—   64 Princes St.
  GLASGOW—   115 Hope St.

Automobile Association (AA-British), 32 Grosvenor Square, London W.1.

British European Airways, Dorland House, Lower Regent Street S.W.1 (370-5411)

Royal Automobile Club (RAC), 83 Pall Mall, London, S.W.1.

Thomas Cook & Son:
  LONDON—   Berkeley St. (central office).
  BIRMINGHAM— 99 New St.
  EDINBURGH— 126 Princes St.
  GLASGOW—   15 Gordon St.
  LIVERPOOL— 75 Church St.
  MANCHESTER— 79 Market St.

Tourist Information Centre, 64–65 St. James's St., London, S.W.1. (629–9191)

United States Embassy, 1 Grosvenor Sq., London, W.1. (499–9000)

What You Should Know About Britain 45

Newspapers and Magazines. Britain offers a tremendous number of daily and weekly publications for every taste. The prime newspaper (but with far from the greatest circulation) is certainly *The Times*. It used to be so conservative in make-up that it printed only a mass of what the British call "small ads" on its front page instead of news. Recently, *The Times* changed all that, and now it allows not only news but sometimes even block capital headlines on its front page. But its ties to the "Establishment"—the worlds of government, finance and society—remain.

Otherwise, there is the Tory *Daily Mail*, or the news-packed *Daily Telegraph*. A reliable and well-written paper is the *Guardian* which has a slightly Liberal Party orientation. *The Daily Express*, a keep-Britain-great sort of paper, is lively and full of exposures—political and otherwise—but is perhaps less interesting to the American visitor. The *Sun* is strongly left-wing, and closely follows the workings of the Unions. These are all morning papers, and they are followed around noon by the *Evening News* and the *Evening Standard*, which often seem to carry more gossip than news.

On Sunday, the three most sober and reliable papers are the *Sunday Times* (no relation to *The Times*), the *Observer* and the *Sunday Telegraph*. The other Sunday papers, such as the *Sunday Express, Sunday Mirror, The People, Sunday Citizen*, etc., are short on news and heavy on special articles of little interest to the tourist, except as a study of folkways and mores. The *News of the World*, with the largest circulation of any newspaper in the world, is a typical British Sunday institution, whose emphasis on murder, sex and vice will come as a surprise to the uninitiated visitor.

A number of estimable weekly political magazines, such as the *New Statesman*, the *Spectator*, and the *Economist* are published in Britain. These cover not only the news of the week, but devote sections to important critical notices. The *Times Literary Supplement* and the *Financial Times* admirably cover their special provinces every week.

Place Names and Pronunciation. Americans find many of the British pronunciations of their place names both amusing and perplexing. There is no easy way to explain these things, and you have to learn them by ear. There are a few obvious special pronunciations which most Americans probably know, such as "Barkley" for Berkeley, "Hoburn" for Holborn, "Mallibone" for Marylebone, "Totnum" for Tottenham, "Grovner" for Grosvenor, "Marshbanks" for Marjoribanks, "Lester" for Leicester, etc. Here are a few hints: Say "Edinboro," for Edinburgh: say "Cissester" for Cirencester; say "Annik" for Alnwick; say "Chumley" for Cholmondeley; say "Barkshire" for Berkshire; say "Hartford" for Hertford; say "Gloster" for Glouces-

The Derby, at Epsom Downs

ter; say "Wooster" for Worcester; say "Darby" for Derby; say "Kikoobrishire" for Kirkcudbrightshire. In general, the British do *not* emphasize the "shire" in county names.

If you hear references to "Liverpudlians," "Mancunians," "Cantabrigians," "Oxonians," "Glaswegians," be sure the talk is not about men from outer space, but about people from Liverpool, Manchester, Cambridge, Oxford, and Glasgow.

Etiquette. The general impression you'll get is that the British are punctilious and not effusive, whereas Americans are more often the opposite. When an Englishwoman says, "You Americans all have such *good* manners," she may not always be intending a compliment. Being reserved, as all the world knows, the British tend to do just enough in the way of manners, and no more. Sometimes they fine it down to the point where it cannot be distinguished from rudeness, at least in their dealings with foreigners. They do not, for example, automatically shake hands when they are introduced, as most Americans and Continentals do. The only guide for the visiting American is his own good taste. In other words, behave as you would at home, but don't lay it on any thicker.

A FEW DO'S AND DON'TS

Do watch traffic carefully your first few days in Britain. It takes some time to get used to cars and buses appearing from what we think of as the wrong side of the road.

What You Should Know About Britain 47

Do stand up in public places when you hear "My Country 'Tis of Thee" being played. It will be the British national anthem, "God Save the Queen."

Do bring your maximum allowance of American cigarettes into the country, if you are a smoker. British cigarettes are not to every American taste.

Do carry your passport when you plan to exchange Travelers Checks. It is required for identification.

Do try to be careful about calling a Scot or a Welshman an "Englishman." If you're starting a sentence with, "Now you English . . ." change it to "Now you British . . ." or "Here in Britain you . . ." The ordinary educated Scot or Welshman won't mind the error, but you never know when you're dealing with a rabid nationalist.

Don't jump waiting lines (called "queues"). The British take a remarkably dim view of such behavior, since they themselves have the queue habit.

Don't take your little problems to the U.S. Embassy or tell your friends to write you there. Embassy personnel have enough on their hands as it is, and as for mail, American Express runs an extremely efficient service for their clients.

Don't bring a big American car with you, if you plan to do extensive touring in out-of-the-way places. The roads will be too narrow, and the gasoline consumption costly.

Don't try to bargain about prices, as you might in parts of the Continent. The British don't expect or welcome bargaining. If it is a question of some expensive art work, or a large quantity of antique furniture or silver, you might try to work out a sensible over-all price with your salesman, but then you would do that at home too.

Don't—above all—don't try to be British while you are traveling in Britain. The natives will much prefer your authentic self to any kind of imitation, good or bad, of themselves.

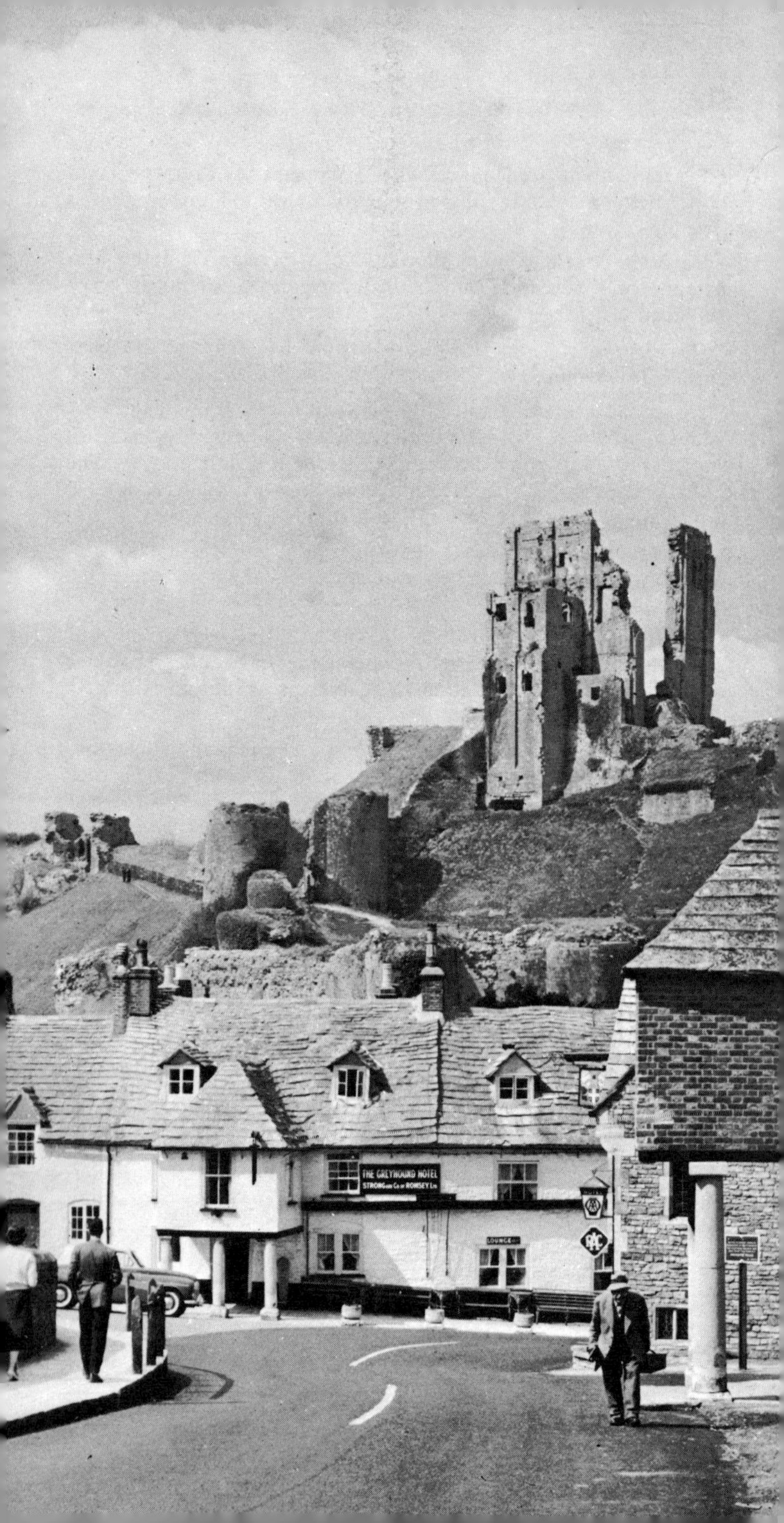
THE GREYHOUND HOTEL
STRONG and Co of ROMSEY Ltd
LOUNGE
RAC

CHAPTER 4

WHAT TO SEE IN ENGLAND

Great Britain is a small country; and simply because it is small you can get to know it even if your time is limited. The distances between towns and rivers and the sights you want to see are small, and sometimes you will be able to enjoy three or four in the same neighborhood in the same day. The details of the picture of Britain presented in the following chapters are obviously not complete; that would take thousands of pages. What has been done is to choose those places and things in Britain which seem most calculated to interest people on a holiday, and then group them in broad informal areas for easy sightseeing. London comes first, naturally, for that is where the majority of visitors receive their first impression.

You will probably discover that you have already been prepared for London and the countryside. British writers have always had such a genius for creating the sense of place, that you experience—when you look at the Yorkshire moors around the Brontë home, or Wordsworth's melancholy Tintern Abbey on the River Wye, or the many old inns peopled by Dickens—that odd yet pleasant shock of recognition.

The visitor here is further helped by the strong feeling the British have for their past; they like to preserve, even exploit it. They don't have our mania for tearing down buildings because they are old, but rather cherish them for their continuing history. Throughout the nation there are many villages where the houses and inns look exactly the way they did in medieval days; and in the town of Bath, for instance, there are still the remains of the elegant thermal baths that the Romans built here. The English use Bath as their favorite spa. Because their own past is so alive to them, they are eager to

The face of England: castle village, and inn.

share it. When you stop in any of the historic spots, especially in the country, try asking questions of the village people. You will be amazed at their storehouse of local lore.

Off the main roads it is astonishing to discover how much real country is still left in the heart of England. To come across great open expanses in the craggy wastes of northern Scotland seems only natural; to find *New Forest,* a wooded tract of some 93,000 acres, just ten miles out of Southhampton, is a wonder. It is still as unspoiled as when William the Conqueror enclosed it for his own pleasure in the 11th century.

The special beauty of Britain lies in the small towns. The larger industrial cities have drawn away the growing population, leaving the villages in serene perfection. Traveling from one county to another, you marvel at the great variety in so small a country. You might expect Wales to be very different from England, but the fascinating thing is to find such marked differences within England itself. Moving from the soft gardenland of Kent to the bleak moorlands of Yorkshire, one can understand why it's said that English counties are countries in themselves.

One of the strongest forces for keeping the sense of the treasured past alive all over Britain is the system of the National Trust, whereby the government helps to keep going more than one hundred historic houses that would otherwise crumble away or be pulled down for developments, because their owners can't afford the taxes. These great houses—many of them occupied by the same families since the 13th or 14th century—are open to the public. There you do not find the cold formality of a museum, but rather the charm of lived-in homes. (You might glimpse the lady of the house carefully mending the ancient silk hangings of the castle.)

And one last word before you set out: the social center of the small town is the local inn—even the tiniest village has one. Try the hospitable door of the English inn as the quickest way to meet and get the flavor of the people at their most relaxed.

LONDON

Whether it is really the largest city in the world or not, whether it is actually "the hub of the universe" (as the British like to think of it) or not, London is beyond any doubt one of the most interesting, civilized, and important cities in the world, and cannot be bypassed when visiting Britain. Your stay there may be short or long, but stay there you must. While it is true that the visitor who knows only London has missed a great deal that is essential to Britain, the opposite is also true. Cosmopolitan though it may be, London is a thoroughly British creation, immensely rewarding to anyone who enjoys travel.

Remember that it's a city that has been built up gradually in the course of many centuries, without any plan. Its streets are winding,

What to See in England   51

mainly narrow, and change their names at will. The architecture is extraordinarily eclectic, representing many periods—some good, some bad. There are three architects who have left the strongest mark on London: Inigo Jones, Sir Christopher Wren, and John Nash. Any building designed by one of them merits your attention.

You may find London sooty and unlaundered; most big cities with teeming populations are. In the case of London, the patina caused by smoke and fog and rain has only added to its beauty. It feels well worn and comfortable.

It probably won't surprise you to find that London is really a cluster of distinctive neighborhoods, easily separated in the abstract but all somehow flowing together to form the whole. Some of these areas are described below.

The City, nominally independent from London, with its own charter and Lord Mayor, is the financial district of London. Since it is the original settlement of London, the City is full of Anglo-Saxon and Norman traces. It is crowned by Wren's greatest achievement, *St. Paul's Cathedral.* The original St. Paul's (of which John Donne was dean in the 17th century) was severely damaged, along with so many other buildings, during the Great Fire of 1666. Replacing it gave Wren his most glorious opportunity, and he personally supervised every stage of the building operation from 1675 to 1710. The dome was a brilliant feat of engineering in its time and the church is noted for its beautiful Baroque proportions. You can ascend not only to the Whispering Gallery to test its mysterious acoustics, but also to the ball atop the spire over the dome, from which there is an extraordinary panorama of London. St. Paul's went miraculously untouched during the late bombing, even though the neighborhood all around it was almost completely flattened.

West End. Roughly what we would call the "downtown" district, the most modern part of the city where you are likely to spend most of your time, the West End is not easy to define. Sometimes it is taken to mean all of London west of the City, and sometimes it signifies a smaller area: a circle about a mile in diameter with Piccadilly Circus as its nucleus. In any case it is that part of London which includes the theater and shopping areas, Soho and Mayfair. Shaftesbury Avenue, off Piccadilly Circus, corresponds to New York's Broadway, being the theater center, just as Leicester (pronounced "Lester") Square is the movie center.

Soho is a small neighborhood bordering Shaftesbury Avenue that contains several excellent foreign restaurants and has brought a somewhat exotic flavor into the heart of London ever since the French Huguenots settled there in the 17th century. But if you have a glamorous notion of it, you'll be disappointed: it's rather shabby, with narrow congested streets.

Mayfair is fashionable and elegant, a section of luxurious hotels, handsome Georgian town houses, quality shops, banks, tourist

London: the Thames and St. Paul's

offices, and the American Embassy in Grosvenor Square. The most famous shopping focus is Bond Street, but Mayfair also includes Piccadilly, Regent Street, Savile Row, the Burlington Arcade, and (several rungs lower) Oxford Street. One of Mayfair's curiosities is Shepherd Market, an old-fashioned miniature village of food stalls, pubs, and modest private dwellings that contrast with the opulence of the rest of Mayfair.

St. James's is preeminently clubland, art galleries, and service flats. It also includes *St. James's Park*, which has the charm of a bit of wooded country within the city, complete with a special island for "ornamental waterfowl." Along *the Mall*, a wide thoroughfare perfect for state processions, stand the impressive piles of Carlton House, the pleasing brick *St. James's Palace* built for Henry VIII and the official residence of the sovereign until Queen Victoria moved to Buckingham Palace, and Clarence House where the Queen Mother lives. At the western end of the Mall is *Buckingham Palace*, the monarch's present London home, an edifice more dignified than handsome which was bought by George III from the Duke of Buckingham and rebuilt by John Nash in the time of George IV.

Green Park, just west of St. James's, is a peaceful area of trees and green lawn where sheep still graze and office workers relax during the lunch hour. *Hyde Park*, the largest of the surprising number of parks that cover the city so delightfully, is famous for its lovely planting and outdoor orators at Marble Arch. It is a favorite with Londoners who come out during the fair-weather months for long strolls, or ride horseback in Rotten Row, sit for hours in the sun, and row or even bathe in the Serpentine.

Whitehall. Southeast of Piccadilly Circus and dominated by Trafalgar Square (famous for its stone lions, Lord Nelson's tall column, the illuminated fountains, and noisy starlings and political demonstrations) is the short wide thoroughfare called Whitehall, where most of the government offices are located, each in its own mansion. Two 18th-century buildings—Nelson's *Old Admiralty* and the *Horse*

Houses of Parliament, Big Ben, and Westminster Bridge

Guards—are especially notable. This street is named for the ancient sprawling *Whitehall Palace* that had been the favorite London residence of Henry VIII and successive monarchs until it was destroyed by fire in the 18th century. The only survival from the old palace was luckily the *Banqueting Hall* (designed by Inigo Jones about 1620), one of the most beautiful buildings in London. Charles I had his head cut off in front of the hall and in his memory a glorious equestrian statue of him now surveys this spot from a little distance north. Opening into Whitehall is the narrow unimposing cul-de-sac of Downing Street, where the Prime Minister resides; across from it are the offices of New Scotland Yard.

Westminster. Parliament Square (at the end of Whitehall) is bounded by the Houses of Parliament on the east and Westminster Abbey on the south. Even before the Norman invasion in 1066, a palace of some sort stood on the site of the present Houses of Parliament (also called New Westminster Palace). William the Conqueror made many additions to it and, up to the time of Henry VIII, English kings lived in it. Only Westminster Hall, originally built by William II (son of the Conqueror) survives from the 11th-century Westminster Palace. The remainder was burned down in the great fire of 1834, and the present Houses were designed by Sir Charles Barry in 1852, a fact which surprises many visitors who are impressed by the building's appearance of antiquity. The most popularly symbolic part of the Houses of Parliament is the 315-foot Clock Tower, famous for the largest and most "authoritative" clock with its 13-ton bell, called "Big Ben" (after Sir Benjamin Hall, Commissioner of Works when it was put up), whose resonant chimes can be heard all over London.

Across Parliament Square, with its statues of Oliver Cromwell, Richard the Lionhearted, George Canning, and Abraham Lincoln, as well as *St. Margaret's,* a small but not to be missed 15th-century church (restored), with the finest stained-glass window in the country, stands *Westminster Abbey.* This is where sightseeing in London begins for most people, where most of the great heroes and poets of England are honored, and where every monarch from William the Conqueror to Elizabeth II (except Edward V and VIII) has been crowned. Its history goes back to an ancient Benedictine monastery before 800, but it is Edward the Confessor who is regarded as the founder of Westminster Abbey in the 11th century. The magnificent building we see today was largely the rebuilding of Henry III in the 13th century, though many later kings kept adding to it. Henry VII's exquisite lacy stonework chapel, built at the east end in the 16th century, is the gem of the abbey. Allow plenty of time for Westminster—the Poet's Corner, the Coronation Stone, the Stone of Scone, the fascinating waxwork museum in the crypt, are among the hundreds of things to see in what is surely the most history-rich spot in all the world.

Marylebone. *Regent's Park*, north of Piccadilly Circus, is one of the largest and most gracious parks in London, with a fine zoo and exquisite flowers in summer. (Queen Mary's Rose Garden is especially delightful.) The Regency terraces on the park's east and south borders are supreme examples of John Nash's architecture. The rest of Marylebone, largely Georgian, is mainly residential and full of doctors' and dentists' offices.

Belgravia, south of Hyde Park, is a residential area as fashionable as Mayfair, with notable mansions and many foreign embassies. A good number of the splendid Georgian houses, too expensive to keep up these days, have been turned into apartments.

Knightsbridge, the area north of Belgravia, is another shopping and hotel area and also contains a cluster of 19th-century museums on Exhibition Road. There are attractive residential squares and streets here.

Chelsea, a neighborhood often called the "Greenwich Village of London," has traditionally been favored by artists and writers. Nowadays, however, there seem to be more upper-middle-class families than Bohemians living there, though you still see plenty of artists and studios. The walks and gardens along the Thames Embankment of Chelsea are extremely attractive. There are some good foreign restaurants, interesting pubs, and antique shops on the King's Road.

Covent Garden, east of Piccadilly Circus but still vaguely "West End," is that busy area of sheds and stalls and trucks where the fruits, vegetables, and flowers (Shaw's Eliza Doolittle hawked hers here) that supply all of London are sold wholesale. The Royal Opera House is here too, as well as Drury Lane Theater. The street called *the Strand* is one of the busiest thoroughfares in London between the West End and the City. Charing Cross Station is located here, and a multitude of shops, restaurants, hotels, and several theaters.

Kensington is a sedate, upper-class family neighborhood and the traditional retreat of retired colonels and refined maiden ladies.

What to See in England 55

It has also become the "scene" for London's young, trendily-dressed population, and now boasts as many boutiques as it does antique stores. Kensington Gardens, really a western extension of Hyde Park, looks much more like the royal private gardens it once was. Nannies and their well-behaved children cluster around the statue of *Peter Pan*. Inside the gardens is *Kensington Palace,* remodeled for William III by Sir Christopher Wren and famous as the birthplace of Queen Victoria and Queen Mary.

Bloomsbury, northeast of Piccadilly Circus, with its spacious squares has traditionally been lived in by serious intellectuals, perhaps attracted there by the *British Museum*, on Great Russell Street. Recently the University of London erected a striking modern building near the museum.

Holborn is a rather anomalous area, largely the domain of barristers, solicitors, and law clerks but also of lower-middle-class families. The four ancient *Inns of Court*, which prepare for the English bar, are extremely charming: Gray's Inn; Lincoln's Inn; and the ancient Inner Temple and Middle Temple, whose gardens face the Thames. The Temple derives its name from the Knights Templar, the medieval chivalric order. Parts of the Temple date from the 12th century, the Middle Temple Hall from the time of Elizabeth I when Shakespeare himself acted in his plays there. If you take an hour or so off to meander through the gardens of the Inns you will be rewarded by a sense of traditional tranquillity and an appreciation of the best aspects of British life.

Hampstead Heath, 5 miles north of central London, is an extensive and unspoiled tract of countryside, popular with Londoners on week-ends. The pleasant old village at the top of Hampstead Hill has long been a favorite residence of artists and writers.

Fleet Street, a continuation of the Strand, is full of literary associations and is the gateway to the City. At the start of Fleet Street is Temple Bar Memorial, western boundary of the City. When the Queen makes her annual ceremonial visit to the City, the Lord Mayor and his entourage make a traditional gesture of challenge here. Most of the large London newspapers have shiny modern offices in Fleet Street; only the *Times* prefers to remain aloof in nearby Printing House Square.

East End. Here is the great dock area of London, as well as a vast section of lower-class dwellings. You won't be likely to explore here much (unless you want to see some real sailors' pubs), except for the *Tower of London*, the finest medieval fortress in England. Built by William the Conqueror in 1087, it was used first as a royal residence, then as a prison, and has had a savage and fascinating history.

Tower of London

SOME SIGHTSEEING SUGGESTIONS

Carlyle's House (24 Cheyne Row in Chelsea). The unpretentious and appealing home of the famous writer and his wife, with interesting personal mementos. (Daily, except Tues., 10 to 1, 2 to 6; Sun. 2:30 to 6).

Changing of the Queen's Guard. The colorful military ceremony which takes place in front of Buckingham Palace weekdays at 11 A.M. and Sun. at 10 when the court is in London.

Changing of the Household Cavalry Guard. Daily ceremony at Whitehall, takes place in front of the Horse Guards building at 11 A.M. (10 on Sun.)

Dickens's House (48 Doughty St. near Holborn). The most complete library of Dickens's books and illustrations, and a museum of portraits, letters, and his personal belongings. (Daily, except Sun., 10 to 12:30 and 2 to 5.)

Guildhall (in Guildhall Yard, off Cheapside in the City). Originally built in the 15th century, rebuilt after the 1666 fire, then damaged again in the 1940 great fire. A patchwork of restorations but interesting nonetheless; scene of many impressive state banquets.

Houses of Parliament (Parliament Square). Visitors admitted on Saturdays and public holidays, 10 to 4:30, if neither house is sitting. To attend a debate apply to your embassy.

Dr. Johnson's House (17 Gough Square, off Fleet Street). Contains reminders of the famous writer and conversationalist, including the attic where he and assistants worked on his great Dictionary. (Daily except Sun. 10:30 to 4:30 or 5.)

Keat's House (Keats Grove in Hampstead). Home of the poet and garden where he wrote "Ode to a Nightingale." Personal portraits, books, and letters. (Daily, except Sun., 10 to 6.)

Law Courts (north side of the Strand). These Royal Courts of Justice are an impressive 19th-century copy of medieval Gothic buildings. Visitors enter public galleries through towers at main entrance. (Mon. to Fri., 10 to 4, when the law courts are in session.)

What to See in England

Madame Tussaud's (Marylebone Rd.). Perennially popular waxworks of famous and infamous people. (Daily 10 to 7, Sat. and Sun. 10 to 6:30.)

The Monument (King William St.). A 202-foot column commemorating the Great Fire of 1666. Splendid view of London from the top.

Old Bailey (Newgate St.). Contains the Central Criminal Court, scene of many famous British murder trials which are public and popular.

Old Cheshire Cheese (Wine Office Court, off Fleet St.). Notable inn, rebuilt in 1667 after the Great Fire, retains the atmosphere of Dr. Johnson and Oliver Goldsmith. Crowded.

Post Office Tower. (Maple St.). The tallest structure in Britain, this new and controversial addition to the London scene offers a spectacular view from the top, and a revolving restaurant as well.

Royal Albert Hall (Kensington Rd.). Sterling example of Victorian architecture at its best or worst, depending on your point of view. The huge amphitheater, roofed with a glass dome, is used for concerts, public meetings, and exhibitions. Opposite is the *Albert Memorial*, a pure-Victorian sculpture group showing the Prince Consort reading a catalogue of the Great Exhibition of 1851!

Tower of London (East End). Open weekdays 9:30 to 6:30 in summer and 9:30 to 5 in winter. Sun. 2 to 5 in summer only (see *East End*).

Trooping the Colour. This most impressive military pageant in London takes place every June on the Queen's official birthday, on the Parade Ground in St. James's Park.

A Selected Museum Guide

British Museum (Great Russell St., W.C.1). Enormous collection of art and artifacts from a staggering number of lands and ages. Much of it is magnificent, much is merely exhausting. On a short visit don't miss the Elgin Marbles from the Parthenon.

London Museum (Kensington Palace, W.8). Interesting models of the historical and domestic life of London from earliest times.

"Museum Land" (Exhibition Rd. and Cromwell Rd., South Kensington S.W. 7). Five first-rate museums are conveniently grouped together: *Natural History Museum*—perhaps the world's finest. *Science Museum*—children (and grownups) are fascinated by the push-button working models. *Victoria and Albert Museum*—largest of the group, devoted to ornamental and applied art. Also *Geological Museum*.

National Gallery (Trafalgar Square). One of the greatest and best-hung collections in the world of European paintings. If you have time for only one museum, this is the most rewarding.

National Portrait Gallery (behind the National Gallery). Interesting paintings and sculpture of every famous (nonliving) British person. (Weekdays 10 to 5, Sat. 10 to 6, Sun. 2 to 6.)

Sir John Soane's Museum (13 Lincoln's Inn Fields, off Kingsway). Fine paintings (especially Hogarth's) ingeniously arranged in the private home of the famous architect. (Closed Sun., Mon. and August.)

Tate Gallery (Millbank, S.W. 1 near Chelsea). Unrivaled collection of British paintings—great Blakes and Turners—and modern foreign painting and sculpture, especially of the French Impressionist school. (Weekdays 10 to 6, Sun. 2 to 6.)

Wallace Collection (Manchester Square in Marylebone). Priceless private collection of art (especially French paintings) in a beautiful mansion. Also important arms and armor. (Weekdays 10 to 5, Sun. 2 to 5.)

OUTSIDE OF LONDON

Richmond (Surrey). A beautifully situated resort on the Thames, just 8 miles from London. (Reached by underground, bus, or— best of all—Thames River boat.) Spacious Richmond Park (2,500 acres), which Charles I had enclosed as a playground for his children, offers a pleasant oasis close to town.

Kew Gardens, the Royal Botanic Gardens in nearby Kew, contain 65,000 different varieties of plants, wonderful trees, and lovely vistas. In spring especially, it's breathtaking. *Kew Palace*, built in 1631, was the favorite home of George III and Queen Charlotte. (Gardens open daily; museums, weekdays 1 to 4:30, Sun. 1 to 5:30.)

Ham House (Petersham, Surrey). Built in 1610; has a unique collection of Stuart furniture. (May-Sept. 2 to 6, Oct.-Mar. 12 to 4. Closed Mondays.)

Hampton Court Palace (Middlesex), delightfully situated on the banks of the Thames, is one of the finest specimens of Tudor architecture. Cardinal Wolsey began it in 1514, but fifteen years later was forced to "present" the palace to Henry VIII. Later additions were designed by Wren for William III, and for over two centuries it was the favorite royal residence. This vast mellow red brick palace is one of the handsomest and most romantic buildings in England; don't miss it. Its celebrated gardens have an ancient and intricate *maze* which is still good fun. (Gardens and courtyards open daily until dusk; State Apartments and picture gallery daily 9:30 to 5:45 in summer, until 3:45 or 4:45 in winter; Sun., 2 to 5:45. Green Line bus or Thames River boat.)

Chiswick House (Middlesex), set in a magnificent park. This villa was built by Lord Burlington in 1725 in imitation of Palladio's Villa Capra near Vicenza. Edward VII lived here as Prince of Wales. (Apr.-Sept. 10 to 6:30, Oct.-Mar. 10:30 to 4. Closed Mondays and Tuesdays. By underground or bus.)

What to See in England

Hatfield House (Hertfordshire). One of the most magnificent Tudor mansions, built by Robert Cecil, first Earl of Salisbury, about 1610, has been the home of the Cecil family ever since. In the West Gardens is a part of the Old Palace where Elizabeth I, as a princess, was imprisoned (1555-58) by her half-sister, Mary. Some interesting personal relics of Elizabeth are preserved here, as well as works of art in the main house. (Weekdays, between Easter Sun. and end of May. Daily except Mon. during July, Aug. and Sept. Hours 12 to 5, and Sun. 2:30 to 5:30. Green Line bus or train from King's Cross.)

Hughenden Manor (High Wycombe, Buckinghamshire). Home of Benjamin Disraeli; a typical example of a Victorian gentleman's country home, contains many of his personal mementos. (Open daily, except Tues. 2 to 6; Sat. and Sun. 12:30–6. Open holiday Mons., but closed the next day. Closed Jan. Green Line bus.)

St. Albans (Hertfordshire) is a 2,000-year-old town, named after a Roman soldier who was the first Christian martyr in Britain. Its *Cathedral* is one of the earliest Norman churches in England. The *Verulamium Museum* contains relics from the original Roman city, and there are also remains of a Roman theater, the only one in England. *The Fighting Cocks Inn* is the oldest inhabited house in the country.

Greenwich, about 5 miles down river from central London, contains the Royal Naval College. Here also is *Queen's House*, designed in 1618 by Inigo Jones for the wife of James I, Anne of Denmark, and now forming part of the *National Maritime Museum*. (Daily 10 to 6, Sun. 2:30 to 6.) On the highest hill in Greenwich Park (beautifully laid out for Charles II by Le Nôtre) stand the old buildings of the *Royal Observatory* which have moved to Herstmonceux Castle in Sussex on account of the London smoke. But prime meridian of longitude and official mean time is still reckoned from Greenwich, and visitors like to watch the time-ball descend precisely at 1 P.M. The terrace beside the observatory gives a splendid view over London. Planetarium shows at stated hours. And don't miss the brand new Neptune Hall. (Train from Charing Cross or Thames River boats.)

Seventeenth century mansions near London: Ham House and Hatfield

Jane Austen's house at Chawton, near Winchester

THE SOUTH COAST

This somewhat arbitrarily divided area, just south of London, comprising the counties of Kent, Surrey, Sussex, Hampshire, and the Isle of Wight is sometimes spoken of as *The Weald*, a reminder of the times when it was wild wooded country. Though it is by now highly settled, there are still a surprising number of forests and heaths. Just a few miles off any of the main highways you come upon small villages and secluded streams that make it hard to believe London is only half an hour or so away by electric train.

Surrey. Since this county is within easy commuting distance of the metropolis and does indeed furnish a great deal of its manpower, you might think it merely an extended suburb. This is a mistake, because Surrey has splendid moors and loses any suburban characteristics as soon as you get off the main roads.

Only about 20 miles southwest of London is the old market town of **Dorking,** on the edge of the Vale of Mickleham. Close at hand are *Betchworth Park*, with its unique triple avenue of lime trees, and *Box Hill*, a lovely spot with box trees, where George Meredith lived. Scattered throughout this area of stately trees are charming and surprising hamlets with names like Friday Street, Christmas Pie, Abinger, and Pennypot.

Guildford, on the River Wey, the county town of Surrey, whose history goes back to King Alfred, has the most charming and steepest High Street in England, lined with ruins of a castle and ancient and picturesque houses. Look for the old Guildhall, which has a clock dated 1683 projecting way over the street and for Guildford's interesting old churches. Lewis Carroll lived in this town and is buried in the Mount Cemetery.

A few miles southwest is *Loseley House*, a fine Elizabethan mansion, where Elizabeth I and James I used to visit. Among its works of art and period furniture are cushions embroidered by Elizabeth I. Surrounded by parkland. (Open June-Sept. Fri. and Sat., 2–5.)

What to See in England

Five miles south of Guildford is yet another attractive market town on the river Wey, **Godalming**—birthplace of James Oglethorpe, who founded the state of Georgia. While in the vicinity visit the *Winkworth Arboretum*, 60 lovely acres of trees and flowering shrubs; and flower lovers should stop at Ripley on their way from London to Guildford to enjoy English gardening in all its aspects, for there the Royal Horticultural Society cultivates 200 acres of beautiful gardens. (Open weekdays 10 to 7:30.)

All along the Portsmouth Road, which divides Surrey down the middle, are interesting old inns, such as *The Talbot* at Ripley and *The Crown* (13th century) at Chiddingfold—the oldest inn in Surrey. Near the village of Chiddingfold are also some 400 acres of wild heaths and moorland (Milford Common and Witley Common), close enough to London to afford perfect picnicking.

Just inside the Hampshire border lies the dramatically situated resort called Hindhead, which offers panoramic views. An excellent area for walking, it has *The Devil's Punchbowl*, a favorite bit of unspoiled countryside, nearby.

Kent, called the "Garden of England," gives a comforting impression of trim, small-scale countryside with fertile orchards, fruit farms, and hop gardens. This south coast county was where the Romans first set foot on the island; here the Saxons invaded, the first English church (St. Martin's, in Canterbury) was erected, and the "bomb-alley" of the German bombers heading for London passed directly over Kent. Canterbury will be your main object; it can be approached by either Rochester or Maidstone, both of them interesting cities in their own right.

Rochester, only 28 miles east of London, on the Medway River, has enormous historical interest, dating as it does from Roman times. The Cathedral, developed from a Saxon church of about 600, when the first English bishop was ordained by St. Augustine. The present elegant building is mostly of Norman origin; the elaborately carved west front is especially famous. Other buildings worth seeing are the fine Norman castle, the Elizabethan Eastgate House (now a museum), the Poor Travellers' House, and several old coaching inns. Keep Charles Dickens in mind, for he lived and wrote about this area and you will see many signs of him.

Down river from Rochester is the great naval base of *Chatham*, and 4 miles to the west is *Cobham Hall*, an Elizabethan architectural gem with famous gardens. In the ancient picturesque village of Cobham the *Leather Bottle Inn* looks pretty much the same as it did when Dickens sat there and wrote about Mr. Pickwick and his fellow lodgers at this inn.

Maidstone, the county town of Kent, lies in the midst of hop fields and orchards and has several notable buildings in its environs. One mile north is *Allington Castle*, a moated building of the 13th century

62 Britain

(by appointment only). About 4 miles to the south lies *Boughton Monchelsea Place,* an Elizabethan fortress-manor with a wonderful view over a deer park. (Open April to Oct., Sat., Sun., and Wed. during August, 2:15–6.) *Mereworth Castle,* built in 1720 by Colin Campbell, is one of the few remaining villas in England done in the pure classic style of Palladio. (Open daily in Aug., rest of year Wed. only, 2 to 5.)

The town of Sevenoaks is admired mainly because of nearby *Knole,* one of the largest and most famous private houses in England. Home of the literary Sackville-West family, 15th-century Knole has everything that a "stately home of England" should: hundreds of chimneys and a magnificent interior (over 50 staircases) filled with beautiful furniture and art treasures. (Open Wed., Thurs., Fri., Sat. 10 to 12 and 2 to 4:30. Closed Jan. and Feb.)

Of the many historic buildings near the market town of **Tonbridge**, 8 miles south of Sevenoaks, the most notable is the wonderfully preserved superb 14th-century mansion of *Penshurst Place* (5 miles southwest). The Great Hall of 1340 has a rare feature, a hearth set in the middle of the room. Penshurst has fine furniture, and famous 16th-century classical gardens with wide herb borders, described in the poetry of Ben Jonson and Sir Philip Sidney. The house has belonged to the Sidney family since 1552. (Open Easter to Oct. 10, on Wed., Thurs., Sat. and Sun. from 2 to 6.)

The small village of Hever just south of Tonbridge, boasts *Hever Castle,* a 14th-century moated mansion surrounded by lovely gardens, where Anne Boleyn lived and was courted by Henry VIII.

While in this area you should stop briefly at **Royal Tunbridge Wells,** a pleasant inland resort at the border of Kent and Sussex, noted for its medicinal springs or wells for which the town is named.

But it is really **Canterbury** you want to see, that most beautiful of medieval cities, the goal for Chaucer's pilgrims—and thousands of others—since the time of St. Augustine, who, as a missionary from Rome, built a church here in 597 and established English Christianity. Canterbury is still the spiritual center of the country—the See of the Primate of all England. *Canterbury Cathedral* of course is the focus; and it is a sight which never fails to make one stop. More than other cathedrals, it seems to be a part of the town; people pause here in the Close to rest between chores, hardly bothering to think that much of this superb building has been standing there since 1070. You can still see the marvelously preserved Bell Harry Tower, the northwest transept where the saintly Thomas à Becket was murdered. Among the treasures of the historically fascinating church are the 14th-century tomb of the Black Prince, hung with his shield and battle armor, and some early stained-glass illustrating the miracles of Thomas a Becket. The Cathedral miraculously escaped the repeated bombings from Nazi planes.

Elsewhere in the town can be seen remains of the ancient Roman

What to See in England 63

city, St. Martin's Church (restored, but originally 6th-century); the medieval city walls, and the pretty 17th-century Weaver's House on the river with the looms of the emigré Huguenots.

Canterbury is very close to the Kent seashore, where there are a number of popular summer resorts: Margate, Broadstairs, Deal, Ramsgate, Folkstone. The historic Cinque Ports include Dover, Sandwich, Hythe, Romney, and Hastings (in Sussex). Dover on its high white cliffs has special charm and interest because of its famous Norman fortress-castle. On its grounds is the oldest standing building in England, the 2,000-year old *Pharos* or Roman lighthouse.

Sussex, like Kent, saw a great deal of Britain's earliest history. The town of **Hastings** on the channel prides itself on being the port where William of Normandy concentrated his attack on that one history date every English child remembers—1066. The ruins of William the Conqueror's castle are still there, and near it a little fishing community, but Hastings is now a very modern seaside resort. A few miles inland on a ridge where the Battle of Hastings was fought stands the little town called—with more than usual British understatement—simply Battle. *Battle Abbey* was built here by William in thanks for his victory.

Farther east on the coast is **Rye**, once a subsidiary Cinque Port, but now deserted by the sea. This quaint town has winding cobbled streets, many ancient timbered buildings, a lovely parish church with a unique clock, and a medieval inn called "The Mermaid." Henry James had a picturesque cottage here.

In the same area is one of the prettiest villages in Sussex, **Alfriston,** on the Cuckmore River. Once a smuggling center, it still has the 16th-century inn, *The Star*, which was the smugglers' meeting place, and many medieval timbered houses. Nearby is a notable house, *Glyndebourne,* the country home of Mr. George Christie, that provides a beautiful setting for the world-famous and fashionable Opera Festival that takes place there every summer. It is quite a sight to see the Londoners streaming in on the afternoon trains in full evening dress.

"Incredible Indo-Chinese-Moorish..." Brighton Pavilion

64 Britain

A few miles inland from the coast is **Lewes**, on the Ouse River, an ancient town whose steep narrow streets are crowded with historic buildings. It is worth stopping here to see the romantic Norman castle, one of the oldest churches in Sussex, St. Michael's, and the handsome house built for Henry VIII's fourth wife, Anne of Cleves.

Not far from Lewes in the village of Burwash, is *Bateman's*, the 17th-century house where Rudyard Kipling lived among the South Downs he wrote many poems about. The house contains his personal souvenirs and library and is surrounded by attractive gardens. (March-Oct., weekdays, except Fri., 11 to 12:30, 2 to 6; Sat. and Sun. 2 to 6.)

On the coast, south of Lewes, lies the well-known gay resort of **Brighton**. There is much about modern bustling Brighton that seems brash and commercial, but its setting is dignified Regency. It has been a beloved British resort ever since George IV first came here as Prince Regent because his doctor prescribed its bracing air. There are still some spacious squares and terraces, fine Georgian houses—though most of these now offer "bed and breakfast." The most distinctive attraction of Brighton, however, is the *Royal Pavilion*, an incredible Indo-Chinese-Moorish palace of peculiar charm, built in 1787 by the great architect John Nash for the Prince Regent. The fantastically decorated State Apartments have been kept intact. (Open daily, including Sun., Oct. through June, 10 to 5; July through Sept., 10 to 8.)

Arundel Castle, 4 miles north of Littlehampton, is the home of the Duke of Norfolk, premier peer and Earl Marshal of England. This imposing and historic castle goes back to the early 12th century, though it was much altered later. One of the great showplaces of England, it contains rare paintings and furniture. (Mid-Apr.—mid-June: Mon.-Thurs. 1 to 4:30; mid-June—mid-Sept.: Mon.-Fri. and Sundays in Aug. 12 to 4:30.)

Nearby *Petworth House*, which was rebuilt by the 6th Duke of Somerset in 1696-96 to incorporate a 13th-century chapel, has a magnificent collection of paintings, including some of the local landscapes that Turner painted when he was a guest at the house. It also has a supreme art treasure in the "Leconfeld Aphrodite"—one of only two works definitely ascribed to the great Greek sculptor Praxiteles. (April-Oct., Wed., Thurs., Sat. 2 to 6.)

To the west, and just in from the coast, is the delightful cathedral city of **Chichester**, which was founded by the Romans. Its early Norman Cathedral has been described as "a poem in stone," and Chichester also has an extremely beautiful Market Cross. Priory Park, the Tudor St. Mary's Almshouse, the Guildhall, and the old city walls are worth your attention.

To the north of Chichester is the odd yet dignified three-sided ancestral home of the Duke of Richmond and Gordon, *Goodwood House*. Designed in 1780 by a combined team of the 3rd Duke and

What to See in England 65

the architect James Wyatt, it is a remarkable example of Sussex stonework. Inside are many fine pictures and a unique collection of Sèvres China. (May-Sept., Wed. and Sun., except July 2, 23, and 30.) On the Duke's property is the Goodwood Race course, scene of one of the most fashionable meets in July.

Hampshire. Your first stop will normally be **Winchester**, which is not only one of the loveliest and most unspoiled of English cities but has the added distinction of having been the first capital of England in the 9th century, long before London. As you might expect, it is even more crammed full of history than the other historic towns in the south country. It was at Winchester that King Alfred planned his campaign against the Danes, and there that he was crowned and founded a great center of learning. Wandering around the ancient streets and buildings and medieval rampart walls is a delightful way of absorbing English history. The Cathedral of Winchester was built by the Normans in the 11th century, and besides its architectural beauty, is noted for being the longest church in England. Among its art treasures are the magnificently carved altar screen, the Norman baptismal fount, the burial chests of Saxon kings, and rare medieval wall paintings. Among those buried here are the novelist, Jane Austen, and Izaak Walton, the father of all compleat anglers, who did his fishing on Winchester's fine trout stream, the River Itchen. In the little churchyard beside the Cathedral lies St. Swithin (King Alfred's tutor), who was first buried—against his wishes—in a splendid tomb inside the church, whereupon it rained for 40 days until they moved the saintly man outside. This is the origin of the belief about having rain for 40 days if it rains on St. Swithin's Day, July 15.

Other intensely interesting places around the city are: *The Great Hall*, which is all that remains of Winchester Castle, just outside the medieval West Gate of the old city wall. Here you can see King Arthur's *Round Table*, with places marked off for his 24 knights. Here also are the atmospheric grounds and cloisters of Winchester College, opened in 1382, the oldest of England's great "public" schools for boys. One mile to the south is the superb Hospital of St. Cross, founded in 1136 as an almshouse; it is still dispensing Christian good will in the form of its traditional "Wayfarer's Dole"—a roll and a glass of ale to all comers.

Surrounding Winchester are many old-world villages, among which Chawton is one of the nicest. Here is *Jane Austen's Home*, which was recently turned into a museum and contains the beloved novelist's writing desk, family portraits, and many personal items. (Daily, including Sun., 11 to 4:30.)

The great port of **Southampton**, to the south, is where many Americans first set foot in England and usually stop only to see the *Mayflower Memorial* to the Pilgrim Fathers and the old Tudor House Museum. It is also a fine starting place for the **Isle of Wight**,

Cathedral at Wells, in Somerset

renowned as the sailing center of England, and for its seaside resorts. There are many fine sandy beaches on the island, among them: Cowes (home of the Royal Yacht Squadron and the famous August Regatta), Yarmouth (where there are ruins of a Henry VIII castle), Shanklin (where Keats and Longfellow bathed), Ryde (the best beaches), and Freshwater Bay (lovely scenery and a monument to Lord Tennyson who lived there).

A house of more than average interest is *Carisbrooke Castle*, a very fine medieval castle near Newport, capital of the Isle of Wight. Charles I was imprisoned in the castle and his daughter Elizabeth died in the prison under circumstances that "would have made even a Roundhead feel ashamed of himself." (Weekdays 9:30 to 7 in summer, Sun. 2-7. Closes 4:30 in spring and fall, 4 Nov.-Feb.)

An alternate route to the Isle of Wight is from **Portsmouth**, the great naval base slightly east of Southampton. The major attraction (Dickens's birthplace here is now open to the public) is probably the Royal Dockyard, where Lord Nelson's famous flagship H.M.S. *Victory* is on view. The spot where Nelson fell during the Battle of Trafalgar is marked, and every year on its anniversary the ship is decorated with flags and draped with laurels. The fortress-castle of Portchester, jutting out into the harbor, is where Henry V assembled his troops before the glorious assault on Agincourt.

The area to the west of Southampton is called **New Forest**, though like most such named places in England it was new at the time of William the Conqueror who reserved some 93,000 acres to himself as a hunting area. Today this vast unspoiled area of heath, woodlands, fir plantations, ancient oaks, and also wild ponies (though they will eat out of your hand) still belongs to the crown. It is open to the public, however, and there are few more delightful places in which to walk.

A little farther down the coast is the modern year-round resort of **Bournemouth**. Unlike gay resorts such as Brighton (whose beaches are pebbly), quiet, dignified Bournemouth relies for its appeal on its miles of sandy beaches, picturesque cliffs and gardens, and a fine symphony orchestra.

THE WEST COUNTRY

In these five varied counties—Wiltshire, Somerset, Dorset, Devon, and Cornwall—you begin to feel really distant from London. The West Country is predominantly agricultural; here people speak differently, and their major concerns are local matters. Its sleepy villages and bold chalk downs, rolling hills, lush pasture lands, and cliffside resorts hanging over the sea make an instant appeal.

Wiltshire. The most fitting approach to this small, high-lying county is the lovely cathedral town of **Salisbury**, that Constable loved to paint. Its extraordinary Cathedral was built in a very short period (1220-58), giving it an unusually consistent early English style. The soaring 400-foot spire is the tallest in Britain, and because the Salisbury Cathedral stands in a spacious greensward Close, there are fine views of it for miles around. Outstanding features are the handsome octagonal Chapter House, the superb cloisters, and the cathedral library, which contains one of the four contemporary copies of the Magna Carta. Around the cathedral are enchanting old houses.

Wilton House, three miles west, is the splendid home of the Earl of Pembroke, designed by Holbein and Inigo Jones. The Double Cube Room is unsurpassed: it contains ten pictures by Van Dyck painted in that same room and furniture by Kent and Chippendale. Don't miss the Italian gardens and the 200-year-old lawn with river and bridge. (Open April through Sept., Tues. through Sat. 11 to 5:30; Sun., 2–5:30.)

The most important prehistoric monument in Britain, called **Stonehenge**, lies 9 miles north of Salisbury, near the town of Amesbury. It comprises the mysterous remains of a double circle of huge stones, erected some 2,000 years B.C. and fitted together with amazing precision for that age. Just what the ancient Druids used this site for is still in question—as a burial ground or for sun worship, or perhaps both. But even more mysterious—how did these primitive people set up such boulders (some weighing 40 tons); and since some of the bluestone used is found only in South Wales, how was it transported here from 200 miles away? The place has a beginning-of-the-world lonely quality about it, and the long views of the Salisbury Plains are impressive.

Somerset. This widespread county consists mainly of trim rolling farmland and also a series of high hills with dramatic gorges and the unspoiled expanse of *Exmoor Forest.*

A town with great attraction for the English and visitors alike is **Bath**. Its hot springs were famous even before the Romans—suffering from rheumatism in the northern winters—built elegant thermal baths here, and it is still the most fashionable of British spas. Bath boasts that it is the best-planned town in the land; it is certainly a perfect example of the 18th century at its handsomest. The architects used the natural beauty of its setting high above the River Avon and the honey-colored native stone to create a classical town of spacious buildings, squares, and colonnaded crescents that has rare dignity and charm.

Aside from its sheer beauty, Bath has a wealth of historical and literary memories: Jane Austen and her heroines loved Bath; Mr. Pickwick played whist in the gay Assembly Rooms; and bronze plaques mark the houses where Lord Nelson, General Wolfe, Beau Nash, Queen Victoria, and many other famous people lived. Bath is ideal for leisurely walks; and if you climb Beechen Cliff, across the river, you will get a rewarding vista of the whole enchanting town.

Thirteen miles northwest, on the border between Somerset and Gloucester, is the great inland seaport of **Bristol**. It was from this port 7 miles up the River Avon that John Cabot sailed in 1497 to discover the mainland of America, and for a long time it was the center for the slave trade with the United States. Don't fail to see the Church of *St. Mary Redcliffe*, mainly 15th-century, that Elizabeth I described as "the fairest, the goodliest, and the most famous parish church in England"; and the historic Theatre Royal where the Bristol Old Vic performs. Just outside Bristol is the Clifton Suspension Bridge, a daring engineering feat of the 19th century, which will give you a breathtaking view over the gorge.

Traveling south from Bristol you go through the Mendip Hills, where *Cheddar Gorge*, a pass between perpendicular limestone cliffs boasts some remarkable caves. At the foot of the gorge is the pretty village of **Cheddar**, long famous for its cheese.

You will be heading for the serenely beautiful city of **Wells**. This is Trollope country and also the place W. H. Hudson loved because the rare birds here cheered him when he was lonesome for his South American home. Wells cathedral (12th- to 13th-century), though small, is one of the most impressive in Britain, especially the glorious West Façade, whose six tiers of more than 300 statues comprise the most superb medieval sculpture in the country. The ancient clock, which stages a miniature knightly tournament every time the hour is struck, never fails to fascinate onlookers. Close by, surrounded by a moat, is the *Bishop's Palace*, whose celebrated swans calmly ring a bell when they want to be fed.

Five miles south of Wells is **Glastonbury**, an ancient pilgrimage town full of legends, whose ruined abbey is the oldest in Britain, going back to pre-Saxon days. It is said that St. Joseph of Arimathea brought the holy chalice of the Last Supper here, and that King Arthur and Queen Guinevere are sleeping in the abbey grounds.

If you like curiosities, seek out the village of **Culbone**, surrounded by cliffs and woods, which claims the smallest church (33 x 12 feet)

What to See in England 69

in use in England. It can be reached only on foot or horseback. At a farmhouse a quarter mile from the church, Coleridge composed *Kubla Khan* while in an opium reverie.

Dorset, south of Somerset, continues with the same lush meadow land and rolling hills until its chalk cliffs break upon the English Channel. This is Thomas Hardy's county, of course, and the Gothic-looking stone cottages and the superstitious country people still seem very much the way he described them.

Shaftesbury, in the northern part of the county, is one of the oldest towns in England. The old abbey was founded by King Alfred in 880 and its museum contains interesting relics.

If you turn south en route to Dorchester, you will pass the tiny village of Cerne Abbas, which has an ancient gatehouse, the only remains of a 10th-century Benedictine abbey. On a hill overlooking the village is the prehistoric *Cerne Giant*, a curious figure cut in the chalk, of a man 180 feet high, holding a club. Nobody knows what he signifies.

Dorchester, the "Casterbridge" of Hardy's novels, was built on a Roman site and is crowded with Roman and pre-Roman remains. Of great archeological interest are Maiden Castle, a vast Iron-Age fortified camp, and Maumbury Rings, which is a well-preserved Roman amphitheater.

The Dorset coast has miles of impressive cliff scenery. Swanage to the east, and Lyme Regis, the setting for Jane Austen's "Persuasion," are attractive little resorts with good bathing and pleasant walks.

Devon and Cornwall. When you reach these two counties, not far from London by American standards, you will feel remote, almost as if you were in another country. The weather is warmer and wetter, the scenery embraces both rugged granite cliffs and the soft beauty of palm trees, the coast is dotted with fishing villages of terraced narrow streets that have a Riviera look to them, the earth becomes redder and the people shorter and darker, showing their Celtic strain. You will find yourself using the words "picturesque" and "quaint" time and time again, and selfishly wishing that these villages had not been the delight of tourists since the 19th century. This country can be explored only by car or bicycle; the roads are narrow and often tortuous. The best approach is by way of South Devon to Cornwall, then returning by the route through North Devon.

Exeter, the county seat of Devon, beautifully situated on the River Exe, was badly bombed during the war, but its famous Cathedral was spared. It is a glorious example of "decorative" Gothic of the 13th and 14th century, with fine carvings, a statue-covered portico, a minstrels' gallery, and towers uniquely placed at the end of the transepts. Other things to see in Exeter are the noble Elizabethan

Guildhall, the ruins of William the Conqueror's Rougemont Castle, the Roman Mosaics, and interesting ancient houses in the cathedral's Close. You will enjoy stopping in the souvenir shop of *Mol's Coffee House*, where Drake and his Devon captains met to discuss their defense against the Spanish Armada.

To the west and south of Exeter is **Dartmoor**, a wild and desolate expanse of high land, with masses of granite called "tors," some of them 2,000 feet high. Buzzards and ravens fly overhead, red deer run wild, and the fogs descend suddenly in this perfect setting for "The Hound of the Baskervilles" and a hundred other English detective stories. Dartmoor also has unhaunted areas full of grazing sheep and excellent trout streams. Be prepared for tricky driving conditions on the way down to the coast.

Overlooking the magnificent Tor Bay is the popular resort of **Torquay**, "Queen of the British Riviera," which claims to have the warmest climate in England. It does indeed look like a Mediterranean town, complete to palm trees. On the beach is the historic "Spanish Barn"—where 400 men from the Spanish Armada were imprisoned.

The road along the coast south of Torquay is good and the scenery is extraordinary. You will pass the lovely old seaport of **Dartmouth**, home of many artists and also the Royal Naval College, and the almost tropical resort of Salcombe, with its fine secluded beaches, on your way to **Plymouth**. This great port, which suffered frightful bomb damage during the war, was visited by the *Mayflower* on its journey to America; but, for the British, Plymouth is Drake's town. On the Hoe, a high esplanade overlooking the harbor, a statue to Sir Francis testifies that he was playing bowls here when the news came that the Spanish Armada was approaching. He finished the game.

After Plymouth you are almost immediately in **Cornwall**, with its fascinating coast line of red cliffs and slate-roofed stone cottages that look more Welsh than English. Its history goes back farther perhaps than any other part of Britain: there seems good reason to believe that the Phoenicians and certainly the Greeks had commerce with the ancient people of Cornwall. This is the traditional land of fairy tales and Celtic superstitions.

The best way to get from Plymouth to Cornwall is by ferry; otherwise you have to make a long detour to cross the Tamar River, which divides Cornwall from Devon. Your first stop will probably be *Polperro*, a typical Cornish fishing village in a narrow ravine with sandy coves. This and other delightful villages like Fowey and Mevagissey farther down the coast are quiet ideal places for swimming, boating, and relaxing. But if you push on to Falmouth, one of the larger resorts with a fine harbor for yachting, and around the large peninsula called "the Lizard," you will reach the village of Marazion, where you should stop to see *St. Michael's*

The westernmost edge of England—Land's End in Cornwall

Mount, a picturesque church and castle set on the pinnacle of a rock which looks, from a distance, astonishingly like Mont-St.-Michel in France. At high tide the rock becomes an island, connected to the mainland by a causeway. (Open all year Wed. and Fri.; Mon. also from June to Sept.)

Just beyond, you reach the ex-pirate port of **Penzance**, where you will probably stay if you want to go all the way out to *Land's End*, the westernmost tip of England. This end-of-the-island with its spectacular cliffs has a great sentimental attraction and is almost never free of sightseeing crowds.

The **Scilly Islands**, about 27 miles southwest of Land's End, can be reached from Penzance by boat (usually rough crossing) or by a few minutes' plane ride from Land's End. Only five of the more than 100 tiny islands are populated, and sparsely, but they are justly renowned for their mild climate, superb beaches, and ravishing flower fields, which bloom from April to Christmas.

As you go north from Land's End you come (like the Mother Goose traveler) to old-world **St. Ives**, where artists have settled for a long time because of its picturesque aspects, and visitors come because of its attractive harbor and fine sand beach. This north coast of Cornwall has so many enchanting little villages that you will have to make your own choice. **Tintagel**, farther up the coast, has a special appeal because of its ruined castle where King Arthur is believed to have been born. It is a hard climb up there, but the view of the rocky coast is unique.

You now approach **North Devon**, where the coastal roads are the narrowest and steepest of all, and the scenery is unrivaled. In the charming but overpopular village of Clovelly, for example, the streets are too precipitous for cars or bicycles; everything has to be carried by donkeys. From Clovelly go inland a bit to see the ancient seaport of Barnstaple, in the beautiful Taw Valley, which has a unique 13th-century bridge of sixteen arches.

Northward to the coast are the lovely twin villages of Lynmouth, which lies on the shore, and Lynton, perched on the edge of a cliff above. Aside from being perfect resorts, they make a fine jumping-off place for trips into Exmoor Forest.

Velvet lawns three hundred years old surround the colleges at Cambridge

EAST ANGLIA

This eastern bulge of southern Britain, taking its name from the 6th-century invading Angles, covers the counties of Essex, Suffolk, Norfolk, and Cambridge. It is low-lying country with dikes and canals that make it look somewhat like Holland. Sparsely populated and less modernized than other parts of the island, it has great character and charm.

The most interesting town is naturally **Cambridge**, where fortunate students from all over the world spend their time in buildings of medieval splendor. Unlike Oxford, which has been engulfed by its industrialized city, Cambridge exists only for its university (though the surrounding truck-farmers come to market here). All of Cambridge has great architectural beauty, but the jewel is *King's College Chapel* (15th century), one of the most perfect buildings in the world. The choir with its trumpeting angels, the exquisite fan vaulting, the stained-glass windows, and the lofty spires all contribute to its transcendent beauty.

You should wander through Cambridge as if you had unlimited leisure, for you will also want to see some of the other colleges: Queen's, Jesus, St. John's, and Trinity—to pick only a few of the 21 that make up the university. Don't neglect a stroll along "The Backs," the lovely tree-shaded lawns and gardens running from the backs of the colleges down to the peaceful River Cam. During the so-called "May Week" (held in June), with the College Boat Races, Cambridge is at its liveliest. To get a wonderful panoramic view of Cambridge, go somewhat south of the town to the low Gogmagog Hills.

The historical town of **Ely**, standing high on the west bank of the Ouse River (15 miles north of Cambridge), invites a visit, if only for the superb Ely Cathedral, which dominates the low fen country lying around it. The delicate lacy cathedral was begun as early as 1083, and the Gothic Lantern Octagon crowning it is a unique and beautiful structure. The town has proud associations with the last-ditch stand of Hereward the Wake against the Norman invaders (1071) and a number of interesting buildings along its river front.

What to See in England 73

The fens to the north are a strange, isolated region in which you find a variety of unusual wildlife.

In this same area is Newmarket, which has been the racing center of England since the time of James I. About 14 miles farther east stands an ancient Suffolk town that takes its name from St. Edmund, last king of East Anglia, who was martyred here by the Danes when he refused to renounce his faith. Though not well known to travelers, **Bury St. Edmunds** has unusual medieval monuments: its Norman tower, majestic Cathedral, and the vast ruins of an old abbey right in the middle of town, where villagers walk in the serene grace of the rose gardens.

Because **Colchester** (in Essex) was one of the first Roman colonies in Britain, it bristles with historical associations. It was the seat of Shakespeare's King Cymbeline about 40 A.D. and was successfully stormed by the heroic Queen Boadicea in 62 A.D. before she was finally captured by the Romans. In a lighter moment it was home to "Old King Cole" (of Colchester). Its historical monuments, such as the Roman city walls, the Norman castle, and the ruined church of St. Botolph's Priory were often painted by Constable. Today the city is renowned for its roses and oysters.

The bulging coast of East Anglia is studded with important ports as well as modest but interesting seaside villages, less crowded by bathing parties than the south coast of England. Inland a large thriving port on the River Orwell is **Ipswich**, Suffolk's county town, in which you will find the 16th-century Ancient House and Christchurch Mansion, but where many people look only for *The Great White Horse Hotel*, scene of Mr. Pickwick's memorable nocturnal adventures. The Anglo-Saxon hamlet of Dunwich, once a port, is a fascinating example of the way the North Sea eats away at this coast.

The Peggotty family of "David Copperfield" have assured the fame of Yarmouth, or more properly, **Great Yarmouth**, the main town and most active fishing port of Norfolk. It is also a popular resort, a characteristic feature being the old "Rows," a series of narrow covered lanes leading down to the sea front.

Yarmouth is one of the gateways to the *Norfolk Broads*, or *Broadland*, 200 miles of interlocked lakes and streams, where you can hire a boat for an ideal vacation of smooth-water sailing, swimming, fishing, and the sheer relaxed enjoyment of agreeable scenery.

Inland from Yarmouth is the Norfolk capital of **Norwich**, notable for its cathedral, a 12th-century structure with flying buttresses and lovely soaring spire, and its huge Norman castle, which now houses an exceptionally fine museum.

North of Norwich visit the romantic and beautiful 17th-century brick mansion *Blickling Hall*, belonging to the Marquess of Lothian. Legend says Anne Boleyn was born here, and her headless ghost visits her old home regularly. There are handsomely furnished state rooms and gardens and park in the style of "Capability" Brown. (Open Apr.-Oct. 8 Tues.-Sun. 2 to 6; Gardens open May 28-Sept. 11 to 6.)

The Queen's country house, *Sandringham Hall*, is in this part of Norfolk; and *Holkham Hall*, the famous country home of the Earl of Leicester, is near Wells on the coast. It is a remarkable mansion in the style of Palladio with beautiful furnishings. (June-Sept. 20, Thurs. 2 to 5; also every Mon. in July and Aug.)

THE MIDLANDS

Ask any ten Englishmen what "The Midlands" means, and you are likely to get ten different answers. It is a catch-all phrase, popularly used to account for the central section of England, and includes a great number of small and large counties differing sharply in their character. The great industrial power of Britain is concentrated in the Midlands, and with it the ugly Victorian towns that inevitably go hand in hand. But the Midlands also include the scenic Wye and Severn valleys, the lovely sleepy hamlets of the Cotswolds, the mountainous Peak District of Derbyshire, the farm lands of Herefordshire and Shropshire and, most important, Oxford and the Shakespeare country.

Windsor, only 22 miles from London, makes a good start for exploring the Midlands. The town is on the Thames in the county of Berkshire and is notable of course for *Windsor Castle*, where British sovereigns have been living for almost nine hundred years. William the Conqueror started a castle there, but most of its present appearance stems from the time of Henry III (13th century), and the extensive renovations of the 19th century, particularly Queen Victoria's. The more impressive aspects of the Castle are St. George's Perpendicular Chapel, the Albert Memorial Chapel, and the magnificent views from the North Terrace and the Round Tower battlement. The art collection is famous for its Van Dycks and Holbein portraits. (Open every day when the Court is not in residence, 10 to sunset. State Apartments weekdays only, Nov.-Feb., 11 to 3; March, Apr., and Oct. 11 to 4; May-Sept. 11 to 5.)

Just across the river from Windsor is *Eton*, the most famous "public" school in England. Founded in 1440, its red-brick Tudor buildings and sweeping lawns make an impressive setting.

There are a variety of other attractive and popular towns along the banks of the Thames between London and Oxford: Maidenhead, Great Marlow, Henley; the most delightful way to see them is to hire a little boat and explore them from the riverside. A few miles downstream from Windsor is *Egham*, on whose meadow of *Runnymede* King John was forced to accept Magna Carta.

Oxford itself (in Oxfordshire county) could easily take up a week of your time if you cared to make a fairly thorough job of it. The present industrial city is too crowded for everyone's taste—but who can resist the handsome colleges of the University? If you visit during the vacations (mid-June to mid-October), sightseeing is easier, but then you miss the characteristic bustle of the University when it is going full-blast, the streets and restaurants teeming with students, and the city traffic always in a jam. "Eights Week," at the end of May, is the time of greatest activity and fun.

Among the colleges not to be missed are *Christ Church*, whose chapel is the Cathedral of Oxford; *Merton*, one of the oldest; *Magdalen*, probably the most beautiful; *New College*, over five hundred years old, with lovely gardens. Spend some time on Oxford's High Street, one of the most fascinating in the world, and look in on renowned Bodleian Library. Most of the colleges are blessed with peaceful cloisters and glistening lawns; especially attractive is the Grove, a deer park attached to Magdalen College, where you can walk along the Cherwell River.

One of the things you might do while in the Oxford area is to visit *Blenheim Palace*, 8 miles north, the vast and opulent 18th-century showplace (sometimes called "England's Versailles") that was presented to the Duke of Marlborough after his great victories. You can see the room where one of his descendents, Sir Winston Churchill, was born, and Blenheim's grounds are superb. (April 6 to July 2 and Sept. 28 to Oct. 28, Mon. through Thurs. 1 to 6; July 6 to Sept. 24, daily except Friday.) Churchill's burial place is at the nearby village of Bladen.

West and north of Oxford is a charming area of secluded valleys, gentle hills and untouched hamlets, called **The Cotswolds**. This region, set mainly in the county of Gloucestershire, and a perfect place for wandering, is full of manor houses, ancient churches, stone cottages and barns. The most popular of the Cotswold towns is *Broadway*, where Barrie created "Peter Pan," but you will probably prefer Stow-on-the-Wold, Bourton-on-the-Water, Chipping Norton, or Upper and Lower Slaughter. A peculiarly harmonious effect is achieved in these villages through the use of a special honey-colored stone. The unofficial capital of the Cotswolds is **Cirencester**, a medieval market town with a fine 15th-century parish church.

A few miles away is ancient **Tewkesbury**, on the Avon River, with a magnificent 12th-century Abbey Church, where the young Prince of Wales was murdered after the battle in nearby *Bloody Meadow* during the Wars of the Roses.

Eleven miles south is the county town of **Gloucester**, an inland seaport (connected to the Severn Estuary by canal), which is an unusual mixture of ancient and modern. Gloucester Cathedral, built from the 11th to 15th century, is noted for its beautiful Norman vaulting and the cloister for its fan tracery. The unfortunate Edward II, (who was murdered with a red hot poker on the orders of his wife Isabella) and a son of William the Conqueror are buried in the Cathedral.

Since the Midlands are so spread out, you have to start off in another direction for the Shakespeare country. **Stratford-on-Avon** (Warwickshire) was once just another quietly charming and isolated village in the heart of England until it was caught up in the 19th-century Shakespeare revival. The associations with Shakespeare are real enough, and often moving (the houses where he lived, Anne Hathaway's cottage, his burial place), the banks of the Avon have a great deal of charm, and the yearly Shakespeare Festival (from April through November) is among the great theatrical events of the world. But the town itself is a kind of tourist trap, with Shakespeare souvenirs everywhere. In summer be prepared for crowds, insufficient hotel space, and Ye Olde English tea rooms.

Stratford is an easy place from which to visit *Kenilworth Castle*, a romantic feudal ruin where the Earl of Leicester, Queen Elizabeth's favorite, entertained her, and about which Scott wrote the novel "Kenilworth." (Open weekdays 9:30 to 7, Sun. 2 to 7 in summer. Closes 5:30 in March, April, and Oct.; 4 from Nov. through Feb.)

From the banks of the Avon, the amazing Norman fortress, *Warwick Castle*, presents one of the most impressive sights in England. It has everything: a moat, dungeons, even a sliding iron gate that is raised each morning and lowered at night. Don't fail to walk through the gardens, where the famous peacocks may put on a show for you. (Open weekdays, April-Sept., 10 to 5:30.)

Eleven miles north of Warwick, the important manufacturing town of **Coventry** (which Lady Godiva befriended) was almost levelled to the ground by bombing during the last war, but it has recovered enough to remain the center of the automobile and bicycle industry. It is being rebuilt as a model of modern town planning. Notice the new Hotel Leofric, the new Cathedral, and the modern Belgrade Theatre: the British are very proud of them.

Birmingham, some 18 miles northeast, is the second largest city in England and the heart of the industrial Midlands. Its highly diversified manufacturing runs the gamut from "ancient" gold relics to airplanes. There are a few handsome buildings, an exceptionally fine art gallery, and a library with the greatest Shakespeare collection in the world. But mainly it is—like most manufacturing cities—quite ugly. Civic center is all being rebuilt.

The old town of **Lichfield** (Staffordshire), Samuel Johnson's birthplace, is about 15 miles north of Birmingham. Dr. Johnson called its inhabitants "the most sober, decent people in England," and Dr. Johnson was usually right. The house where he was born, overlooking the market, is preserved as a museum; Lichfield's other claim to your attention is its elegant lacy 14th-century Cathedral, the only church in England with three spires. The county of Stafford-

What to See in England 77

shire is mainly an industry and mining area: "The Potteries" to the north and the "Black Country" to the south. Smoky, dirty towns are the rule here.

Worcester (Worcestershire), some 20 miles southwest of Birmingham, has other claims to fame besides its sauce and porcelain works. The 13th-century Cathedral is beautifully located on the bank of the Severn River and among its many historic buildings are: *King Charles' House*, where Charles II hid after his defeat in the Battle of Worcester; *Queen Elizabeth's House*, the 15th-century Greyfriars, and the Guildhall. In front of this hall, the intensely Royalist townspeople erected statues of Charles I and II, and over the door a death mask of Cromwell is hung by his ears.

Hereford, the ancient county town, is dominated by its red sandstone Cathedral, an interesting composite of Norman and Gothic styles containing many curious antiques, including a library of chained books. Hereford was the birthplace of Nell Gwyn (her grandson became its bishop); it is noted for wonderful salmon fishing and for Hereford cattle.

The town of Ross-on-Wye is also famous for its delicious salmon, and offers good views of the valley. Symond's Yat, a few miles south, is a beautiful spot where the river makes a spectacular curve on its way to **Monmouth**, the town where Henry V was born. In Monmouth see the handsome and unique 13th-century Norman stone gateway defending the bridge over the Monnow River and the *Nelson Museum*. Within easy reach of Monmouth is the romantic and melancholy remains of *Tintern Abbey*, which inspired Wordsworth's poem of that name.

In **Shropshire**, against the Welsh border, there are a number of appealing places with names like *Much Wenlock*, *Church Stretton*, and *Ludlow on the Cliff*. This is the countryside of A. E. Housman's "A Shropshire Lad," of "Clunton, Clunbury, Clungunford and Clun, the quietest places under the sun."

In **Ludlow**, beautifully situated on two rivers, is the impressive but desolate Ludlow Castle, from which the pathetic little boy princes were taken to be smothered in the Tower of London. Ludlow has a surprising number of well-preserved old timbered houses and a medieval gateway.

Symond's Yat, one of Britain's loveliest valleys

78 Britain

Stokesay Castle, near Ludlow, is probably the finest moated and fortified manor house in the country; it goes back to the 12th century. (Open daily except Tues. 9 to 6.)

The county seat of Shropshire is **Shrewsbury**, situated in a loop of the Severn River that almost encloses the town. Shrewsbury saw many bloody days during the fighting with Wales, but today its quaint old streets with medieval black-and-white houses are very peaceful, and it makes an excellent center for touring the nearby Welsh mountains.

Cheshire County is a peculiar combination of industrial towns and farm lands (where they make the famous cheese) and shares the River Dee with Wales. On the river is the delightful town of **Chester**, founded in Roman times, and today the most medieval looking city in Britain, one of the few with perfectly preserved walls. Chester is also renowned for its fine half-timbered Tudor houses and "The Rows," a unique series of medieval roofed arcades running alongside the first floor of the houses and providing a row of shops above street level.

In the eastern part of the Midlands, the town of **Bedford** (Bedfordshire), on the winding Ouse River, is famed for its beautiful gardens and the jail where John Bunyan wrote "Pilgrim's Progress" while imprisoned there (for preaching without a license). It leads to the so-called "Hunting Shires," where the pink fox-hunting coats bloom: Rutland, Leicester, and Northampton.

In the southern tip of the county near the little town of Banbury (famous for its fine lady who had bells on her toes) is *Sulgrave Manor*, an unpretentious Elizabethan house which Americans visit because it was the home of George Washington's ancestors. It has a little museum and family portraits. (Daily except Wed., 10:30–1:00, and 2:00–5:30; Oct.-March, 10:30–1:00, 2:00–4:00.)

Though it is now a manufacturing center, **Leicester** (Leicestershire)—home of King Lear—is an attractive town with many reminders of its long history, especially the unique Roman Forum and the handsome 15th-century Guildhall.

The bordering county of **Nottinghamshire** is associated not only with Robin Hood but also Lord Byron, whose home, *Newstead Abbey*, is near the town of **Nottingham**. The poet's bedroom and sitting room are kept exactly as he left them; the house has historical, as well as literary, interest. There are also extensive gardens. (April 20 to Sept. 30, daily 2 to 6:30. Gardens open all year.)

Sherwood Forest is hardly the greenwood paradise of Robin Hood's time, of course; the Nottinghamshire coal fields have been encroaching on it. But the northern parts, comprising the so-called "Dukeries"—spacious parks belonging to a group of four dukes—are still lovely, and some of the noble trees from the Middle Ages, like the "Major Oak" or "Robin Hood's Larder" are still preserved.

The county of **Derbyshire**, less defaced by industry, is fortunate

What to See in England

in containing the beautiful *Peak District*. This is really the southern base of the Pennine Range, but it forms a compact area on its own, a popular holiday place of wild moorlands, sometimes as high as 2,000 feet, broken by green and gracious valleys and rocky ravines, through which tumble streams of great beauty. There are good roads here. The most convenient centers from which to see the Peak District are Matlock, Bakewell, and Buxton (a fashionable watering place with excellent accommodations).

There are a surprising number of magnificent mansions in this region, some of the most famous being near Bakewell. *Chatsworth*, home of the Duke of Devonshire, should on no account be missed. Built between 1687-1707, it is remarkable for its size, the most elaborate water-garden in England, and its incredible collection of art and books. (April 4 to Oct. 3, Wed., Thurs., Fri., 11:30 to 4; Sat., Sun. 2 to 5:30.)

The eastern county of **Lincolnshire**, bordered by the North Sea, is an agricultural and fishing area, where the marshes and fens and huge tulip fields make it look very much like Holland. The city of **Lincoln** has a Roman arch over the main road and some other well-preserved remains of Roman Britain. It is graced by a superb Cathedral (11th to 14th century), which stands out impressively on the only hill for miles around. Its three square towers and 12th-century Angel Choir are English architecture at its best. The town's High Bridge still carries a row of old timbered houses on it.

The port and fishing town of **Boston** is full of historical landmarks, and one of them, the 15th-century Guildhall, is particularly interesting to Americans because it was here that the Pilgrims Fathers were imprisoned in 1607 for trying to flee the country. You can see the courtroom and their cells. The graceful high lantern tower of the *Church of St. Botolph* (inexplicably called "Boston Stump") is a famous landmark here.

Country of spires: Lincoln Cathedral and Magdalen College, Oxford

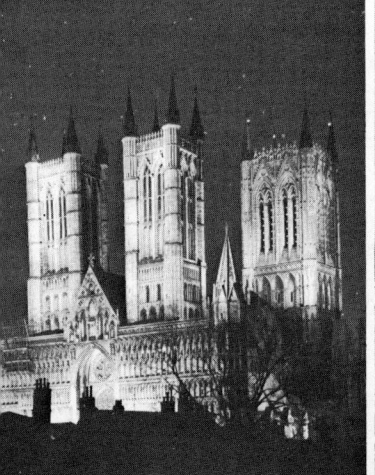

NORTH OF ENGLAND

This area, between the Midlands and Scotland, presents another characteristic, yet quite different, aspect of Britain. The six counties of Yorkshire, Lancashire, Westmorland, Cumberland, County Durham, and Northumberland, though they don't in themselves form a truly homogeneous region, share at least a sense of distance from southern England. Here, in this large stretch encompassing grimy factory towns, popular coastal resorts, haunting moorlands, and beautiful valleys, you sense some resentment of the South, where life is easier, more agreeable, warmer, drier. The North, you soon realize, means hard work. The people here have little time for flattery and social refinements; they do have dash and energy, are great gamblers and proud of their highly developed comic sense. Most of the popular comedians (like Gracie Fields) have come from Lancashire, and part of their comedy derives from the northern accent which southern England snobbishly patronizes. The social caste system is much less rigid in the North: money matters more than pedigree.

For the tourist this part of Britain, excepting the Lake District and the few remarkable medieval towns, does not have overwhelming appeal. In spite of its ancient history of invasion and colonization and struggle, its look is predominantly 19th century: a creation of the Industrial Revolution. But the city of York is different and should not be by-passed. And if you enjoy wild scenery, remember that the North is the one area of England which is really dramatic.

Yorkshire, easily the largest and also the most varied county in Britain, is divided into three Ridings (derived from the old word "thriding," meaning a third). East Riding, less densely populated, is largely agricultural and still echoes to the hunt of the landed aristocracy. West Riding is close-packed and industrial, yet contains the lonely heather moors. In North Riding you find black coal-mining country, but also the lovely hills and dales which are typical of Yorkshire.

The city of **York**, at the junction of the three Ridings and two rivers is so important that it stands by itself, and is not included with any of the Ridings. Next to London, it is probably the most intrinsically interesting city in Britain; indeed, for many centuries it seriously rivaled London as a center of power and influence. It is certainly the finest medieval city in the country, retaining more of its historical appearance than any other. There was a great deal of building in the 18th century, but York has always been conservative, if not backward, and does not tear down its old buildings as readily as most cities do.

The stately *Minster* (or Cathedral Church), largest of English medieval churches, deserves its fame if only for its treasury of 120 superb stained-glass windows. Points of special interest are the richly decorated west front, the soaring central tower, the choir screen, and the exquisite "Five Sisters" window. There are no less than twenty other churches from the Middle Ages in York.

The *City Walls*, which have encircled York since the 14th century, are the longest medieval city fortification in the country. A footpath along the top of the walls makes a delightful place to walk, and York is the perfect city in which to just wander. It has many narrow ancient streets with such names as *Shambles* (once the malodorous street of the butchers), and best of all, one named *Whip-ma-whop-ma-gate*. In your wanderings, don't miss the handsome Merchant Adventurers' Hall, Treasurer's House, the Yorkshire Museum of Roman relics, and the Castle Museum with its unique reconstruction of a typical Yorkshire street of ancient shops and houses.

East Riding. The old seaport of *Hull*, on the Humber River, is the third largest in the country, the place to watch the big fleet of North Sea fishing trawlers coming in. It is also a good place from which to explore the villages and market towns of the East Riding Wolds. You may remember that it was from Hull that Robinson Crusoe started out on his voyage.

West Riding, with the greatest density of population, includes the grimy towns of Bradford, Leeds, Sheffield, Skipton—devoted to the manufacture of wool, yard goods, and steel. These can well be skipped, but not the glorious West Riding moors and dales. Yorkshire moors extend from Yorkshire and Durham right across England westward—to Westmorland and the Lake District. The moorlands are high open country here, ideal for walking and shooting.

The wild and romantic aspects of the Yorkshire moors have of course been forever fixed for us by the Brontë sisters. At **Haworth** you can climb up the hilly Main Street to the stone parsonage house (with garden running down to the graveyard) where the Reverend Brontë brought up his gifted daughters. The *Black Bull* is there too, the inn where their brother Branwell spent too much of his time and his family's money. The parsonage has been turned into a museum, a rather disappointing one; but a stroll in the surrounding lonely moors or a journey to the evocative ruins of Higher Withins —which everyone knows as "Wuthering Heights"—will quickly bring back the intense world of Charlotte and Emily Brontë's novels.

To the northwest of **Wharfedale** begins mountainous country. The most striking and romantic of these heights is *Ingleborough* (2,373 feet), whose caverns, a series of subterranean chambers and passages in the limestone, are unusually fascinating. *Gordale Scar*, near the town of Malham, shows a curious geological freak of nature: a narrow gorge between overhanging cliffs.

Harrogate is a civilized and attractive spa town in this high area, with an international reputation for its 80 curative springs, fine

Brontë parsonage at Haworth, Yorkshire

orchestra and theater, and its famous Valley Gardens. It has luxurious accommodations and is an excellent center not only for sightseeing but for the sporting events that Yorkshire offers in greater abundance than any other part of England. There are two country houses of special interest near Harrogate:

Harewood House and Park is the home of the Princess Royal and the Earl of Harewood. One of the fine Adam 18th-century houses, with magnificent State Rooms, valuable paintings and furniture, and fantastic gardens. (Open Good Friday-Sept. 30, daily, 11–6; and Sun. in Oct., 11–6.

Rudding Park, one of the stateliest Regency mansions, is set in a delightful garden surrounded by woodlands. Beautifully arranged collection of tapestries, pictures, furniture, china, and books. (Open April 2 to Oct. 3, daily except Fri., 2 to 6.)

The charming old town of **Knaresborough**, near Harrogate on the Nidd River, is dominated by its historic 14th-century castle that still looks imposing in its lovely green setting, even though it was, as the English expression goes, "slighted" by Cromwell's army, i.e., reduced to ruins.

About five miles north is the small cathedral city of **Ripon** with a distinctive character of its own. Every evening at 9 o'clock curfew is sounded by the blowing of a horn at the market cross—as it has been since Saxon times. The old Wakeman's House, a unique 13th-century building, still stands in the market square. The *Cathedral of St. Wilfred* is a blend of architectural styles, begun about 1150 and not finished until 1530. It contains the crypt of a 7th-century Saxon church that stood on the site originally, and in this ancient crypt there's a narrow aperture called St. Wilfred's Needle, through which, legend has it, only the virtuous can squeeze. Many buttons have been lost here.

Fountains Hall and Abbey, at Ripon, is a most attractive smaller Renaissance house, with ornamental gardens laid out in 1720. The Abbey, though partly ruined, is one of the noblest monastic buildings in the country (12th century), whose Chapel of the Nine Altars is particularly beautiful. (Open daily, 9:30 to dusk.)

What to See in England

Ripon leads to the Wensleydale Valley (noted for its fine scenery and fine cheese) where you should see *Newby Hall*, a lovely Adam house, with splendid furniture and the most magnificent Gobelin tapestries anywhere outside of France. Extensive gardens. (Open April 2 to Oct. 8, Wed., Thurs., Sat., Sun. 2 to 7.)

North Riding. Of the many Yorkshire seaside resorts, the most attractive is **Scarborough**, on the North Riding coast. This is an old town with great style in a handsome setting: it has a fine harbor, sandy beaches, cliff gardens, parks, and a romantic castle. Along the coast to the north, there are a number of picturesque fishing villages, as well as the quaint old town of Whitby, with its ruined 7th-century Abbey, where the cowherd Caedmon was inspired to write what has come down to us as the earliest poem in English.

Lancashire. This county's only really delightful scenery is concentrated in the north, where it shares the Lake District with Westmorland and Cumberland. The cotton towns need not detain you, unless you have a specialist's interest in them. The so-called "cotton capital," the sprawling, mainly 19th-century town of **Manchester**, is important because it is large, the business center of the North, and has a notable university and 15th-century Cathedral. Surrounding it are the industrial centers of Wigan, Bolton, Blackburn, and Rochdale, known mainly for their manufacturing and successful Association Football teams.

Liverpool is one of the great (though unattractive) ports of the world, the second largest in England, with almost 40 miles of waterfront. It has a striking modern Gothic Cathedral. In the suburb of *Aintree* the *Grand National Steeplechase* is run in March over the most exciting steeplechase course in the world.

Over the historic capital town of **Lancaster** towers the massive Norman *Lancaster Castle* with the famous landmark of John O'Gaunt's Gateway. Its Priory Church contains the most remarkable English wood carving of the 14th century.

Hoghton Tower, near Blackburn, is a famous Elizabethan baronial mansion. It was here that James I during a visit knighted a notable piece of beef as "Sir Loin." (Open daily during Easter week and

Durham Castle and Cathedral overlook the city and the River Wear

84 Britain

Whit-week only; Sun. only during 7 weeks after Easter; mid-June to Sept., Thurs., Sat., Sun. 2 to 5.)

Lancashire has three extremely popular seaside resorts—Blackpool, Southport, and Morecambe—which are all rather outsize Coney Islands. A smaller, quieter, and more attractive resort is Thornton Cleveleys, near Fleetwood, where the boats run to the Isle of Man.

The curious **Isle of Man**, midway in the Irish Sea between England and northern Ireland, is a favorite holiday excursion from Lancashire. Impossibly crowded during August, it is fairly agreeable and interesting at other times. The island was under Norwegian domination from the 9th to the 13th century; now it has a form of Home Rule (more nominal than actual). It has of course given its name to the local tail-less breed of cat. The mountainous terrain is picturesque, and the various towns along the coast (Douglas, Castletown, Ramsey) are well set up for swimming and boating.

The Lake District is England's true vacation country, the county that the Lake Poets have made into official romantic scenery. This corner of 35 square miles is still one of the most beautiful parts of England, an area of mountains and lakes, relatively unspoiled by ancient wars or modern industries, where spring comes late, toward the end of June. There is likely to be a good deal of gentle rain (what is optimistically called "dampening on") right through the summer, but this usually clears quickly, and besides it rarely daunts the hardy British vacationer, who comes here for rambles, rock climbing and bicycling, fishing, and boating on the lakes. The Lakeland is not the place for a hurried tour: it needs perhaps a week. The heart of it is full of picturesque but difficult roads, better for walking than driving, and requires a sense of leisure to be properly enjoyed.

The border town, and largest in Westmorland, of *Kendal*, makes the best center for touring the southern lakes. Many of the houses here were built around a central courtyard, with access only through a single narrow gate—more easily defended during border clashes.

The Lake District: Derwent Water and Lake Windermere

Farmhouse in Cumberland

Levens Hall, a few miles south of Kendal, is a handsome Elizabethan house with magnificent topiary gardens—trees and shrubs, trimmed into the most fantastic shapes. It has a 200-year-old curse—that no son shall inherit from his father—which has so scared the young scions that there has been only one exception. (Open May-Sept. 17. House: Tues.-Thurs. and Sundays, 2 to 5; Gardens 10 to sunset.)

On the west side of Lake Windemere, **Hawkshead** is a former monastic village full of quaint whitewashed cottages, with a 16th-century grammar school where Wordsworth studied for six years. Parallel with Windermere, in Lancashire, is Coniston Water, a good center for rock climbing. John Ruskin's home, *Brantwood*, now a museum, may be visited near the village of Coniston. One of the best-known Lake District beauty spots near here is "Tarn Hows," a little pool in the mountains. The hill called "Old Man," just west of Coniston, offers a popular and easy climb, worth doing for the tremendous view of the countryside for miles around.

One lake already familiar to anyone who has read Wordsworth is *Grasmere*, one of the smallest, though loveliest, just north of Windermere. The poet lived here with his sister Dorothy from 1799-1808 in the house called "Dove Cottage." Thomas De Quincey moved into the cottage when Wordsworth left it for Alan Bank and, later, Rydal Mount near another of the small lakes.

In this southern part of the Lakeland there are countless peaceful little lakes and tarns, less famous and popular, but by the same token less cluttered with tourists than the large ones. You can take your choice of Wast Water (near Scafell Pike, the highest of the Lake District peaks, easily climbed), Esthwaite Water, Loughrigg Tarn, or Stickle Tarn. All are located in hill country of extreme charm and beauty.

For the northern lakes, where the scenery is generally more rugged and grand, the best center is **Keswick** (Cumberland), an old but now lively town where Southey and Coleridge both lived. The largest lake in this region is Ullswater, on which you can take a steamer trip from Pooley Bridge at the north end to Glenridding at the south. It was at Ullsworth that Wordsworth, wandering lonely as a cloud, saw his "crowd, a host of golden daffodils." Nearest to Keswick is Derwent Water, generally considered the most beautiful of all the lakes. It has an imposing mountain background and banks with abrupt crags like "Friar's Crag," a projecting pine-clad rock that is one of the most photographed spots in England. At *Greta Hall* in Keswick, Southey lived and wrote, partly to support Coleridge who also stayed here, as did De Quincey, Wordsworth, Shelley, and Charles Lamb.

Among the other lakes here are Buttermere, Crummock Water, Thirlmere, and Bassenthwaite. Make a point of seeing the loveliest valley in the whole district, *Borrowdale*, which lies south of Derwent Water. Toward the coast from this area is the ancient market town of **Cockermouth**, a pleasant place where Wordsworth fans will want to see the house where he was born.

To the north of the Lake District, within easy reach of it, is **Carlisle**, the county town of Cumberland. It was important in Roman times, and there are many remains of that period, particularly *Hadrian's Roman Wall*, which runs across England to Wallsend. Carlisle had a long and bloody history during the Border Wars and its 11th-century Cathedral, one of the smallest in England, is but a part of what was there before the Scots besieged it in 1645. In the Carlisle Castle, built by William Rufus (son of William the Conqueror), Mary of Scotland was imprisoned before she abdicated in 1568. The dungeon walls are scrawled with carvings made by Scottish prisoners taken during the 1745 rebellion. President Wilson's father was a minister in Carlisle, and his Congregational Church (on Lowther Street) has a plaque recording that fact.

County Durham and Northumberland are often dismissed with little more than a nod as a region you simply pass through between York and Edinburgh. It's true that they're both highly industrial counties, densely populated, full of mining towns, ironworks and ship yards, and that the weather is likely to be dismal. But there are a few compensations which make it worth your while to plan two or three stops along the way.

For example, **Durham** is a charming old city, and Durham Cathedral is one of the great architectural glories of England, ranking in beauty and distinction with Canterbury, Winchester, Lincoln, and Westminster Abbey. It was founded in the year 995, but most of its present Norman aspect dates from the 12th century. Built on high rock overlooking the town, it gives an extraordinary impression of solidity, of what Dr. Johnson called "indeterminate duration." The details of the interior are uniformly magnificent, particularly the colossal pillars with their zigzag molding, the Choir, the Galilee, and the Chapel of the Nine Altars. The Venerable Bede and St. Cuthbert are buried here.

Durham Castle, a stately Norman building standing beside the Cathedral on the River Wear, now houses part of the University of Durham.

What to See in England 87

Toward the west, County Durham shares some of north Yorkshire's moor and dale scenery, particularly in the area of the Tees River. A building of great interest, near the town of Barnard Castle, is the *Bowes Museum*, a rather incongruous looking 19th-century house in the style of a French château, which has a notable collection of porcelain and fine Spanish art, especially El Greco and Goya. (Open March-Oct., 10 to 5:30, Sun. 2 to 5; Nov.-Feb., 10 to 4, Sun. 2 to 4.)

Newcastle-upon-Tyne in Northumberland used to be famous as the eastern pin of Hadrian's Roman Wall, but now it is a large industrial town, known as a shipbuilding and coal-exporting center. Its Cathedral is noted for its remarkable "crown" spire, and the Castle has a 13th-century Black Gate containing Roman antiquities.

Seaton Delaval Hall, near Newcastle, is a masterpiece by Vanburgh, who created Blenheim Palace. (Open May-Sept. Wed. and Sun. 2 to 6.)

While the southern part of Northumberland is full of ugly industrial towns, the northern part and the coast are less populated and very scenic. Off the coast town of Bamburgh are the tiny islands of *Farne*, a well-known bird sanctuary. And slightly north of them, connected to the coast by a causeway, is the strange and legendary island called *Lindisfarne* or *Holy Isle*, which can be reached by boat at low tide. This island was one of the earliest Christian settlements; in 635 St. Aidan was consecrated there as the first bishop. It contains the early romantic ruins of a Benedictine monastery founded about 1080, which formed the background for Scott's "Marmion."

The border country of Northumberland, including the Cheviot Hills and charming Coquetdale, has a great number of fortified castles, which played their part in the seesawing battles that went on there continuously for so many centuries. Especially interesting and impressive are the Castles of *Alnwick* (home of the ancient and present Duke of Northumberland), *Bamburgh* (the oldest, mentioned in the Anglo-Saxon Chronicle as being built in 577), and *Warkworth* (at the mouth of the Coquet).

Bamburgh Castle on the Northumberland coast

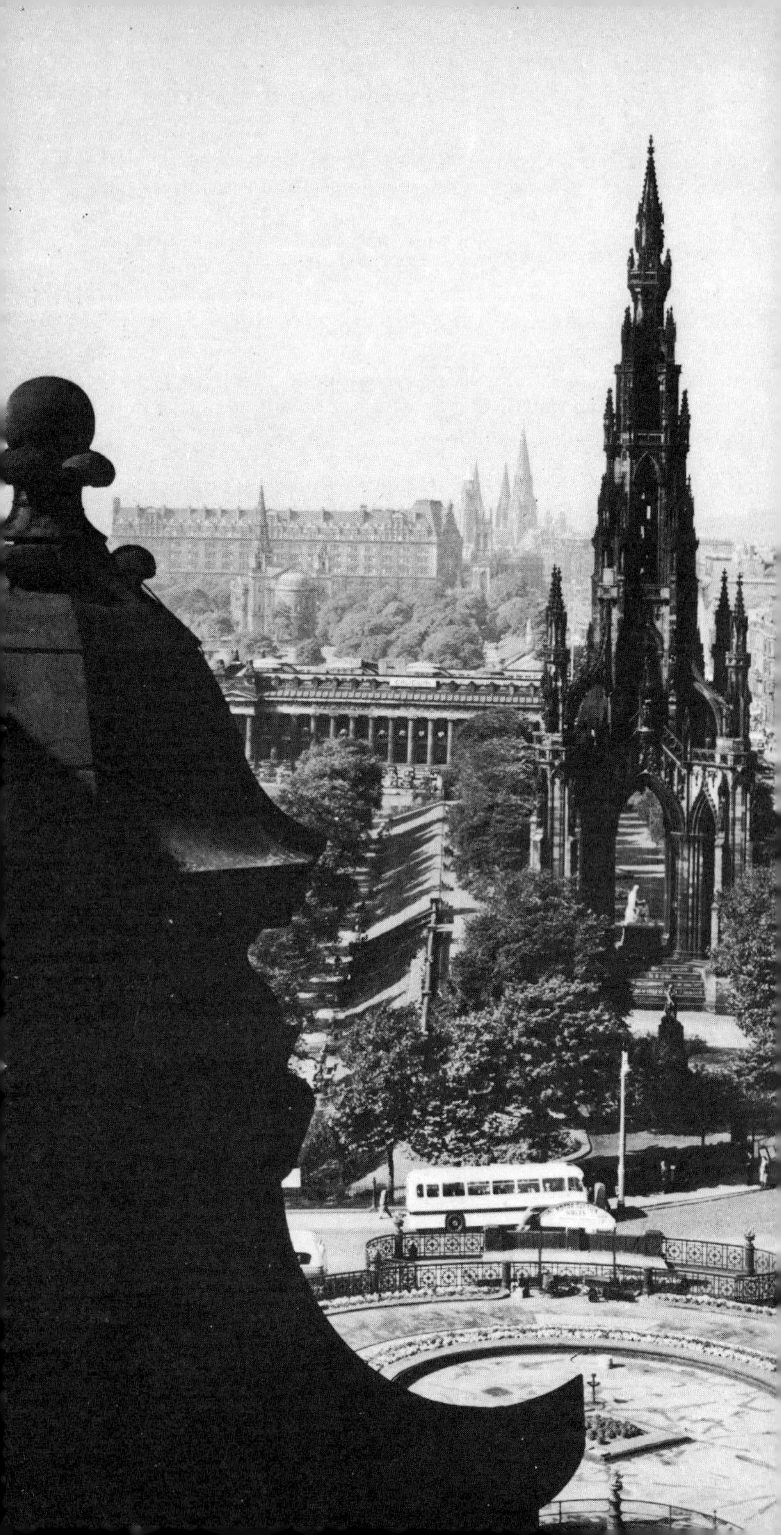

CHAPTER 5

WHAT TO SEE IN SCOTLAND AND WALES

After England, Scotland seems open, almost vast—with long-rolling, gray-green hills crossed only by low stone walls which climb the mountain crests and disappear, seeming to have no end. Occasional bright blue lakes or stone villages are tucked into protecting folds of land and beyond the hills stretch on. This spaciousness is only comparative, of course, for the whole area of Scotland, including the outlying islands, is less than that of either Maine or Virginia. But even so, you must remember, it is a third of the total area of Great Britain. The country is populated only in spots—and there thickly—for large areas either are privately owned or too wild and unprotected to provide for any but the hardiest of highland shepherds. You'll see their flocks roaming the hills, marked by the bright splotches of colored dye which serve as "brands" for identification.

Scotland divides naturally into three sections: the border country, the central Lowlands, where most of the 5,000,000 Scots live and work, and the Highlands—home of the most determinedly Scottish of all Scots—which straggle northward toward Norway and Iceland, the countries they most resemble.

Until the mid-18th century a large part of the Highlands was hardly known at all. A rugged mountain wilderness ruled mainly by clan chiefs who had little contact with the life of either Edinburgh or London (and wanted less), it remained unexplored even at a time when the American colonies had reached a high level of development and prosperity. Remembering that England had been the enemy of Scotland and an acquisitive neighbor and invader, the Highlanders kept to their own customs, organizations, and forms of dress. It wasn't until 1746, when the uprisings around Bonnie Prince

Edinburgh: Scott monument overlooking Princes Street

Charlie became a serious threat to the government in London, that Parliament decided that it was time to disarm the clans, break down the old clan system, prohibit the wearing of the kilt, and rule the Highlands from Westminster.

Scotland differs in many ways from England, as any Scot will proudly tell you. You'll notice first the greater social equality in this northern country. Except in the large, Anglicized cities, class stratification is completely missing. There's a higher degree of self-regard among individuals, and with it a native eccentricity and an inclination to be taciturn. The Scots are polite but slow to make friends—cautious, perhaps, but extraordinarily loyal. Although the feudal aspects of the clan system were successfully destroyed, clannishness is still a lively fact. There are no more important or thoroughly celebrated events in Scotland than the gatherings of great families united by their resounding, ancient names and proudly worn tartans.

THE BORDER COUNTRY

The Border stretches from Gretna Green near Carlisle (Cumberland) northeast to a point just north of Berwick-upon-Tweed (Northumberland). Ruined castles and Gothic skeletons of abbeys stand as evidence of the plunder and destruction which centuries of battle brought to this ancient no-man's-land between England and the Scots.

Jedburgh, up the valley of the Teviot River, is typical of the towns you'll come upon in the border area. The Norman Abbey was founded c. 1143 and destroyed by the English during the wars of the 16th century. Nearby are houses once occupied by Burns, Wordsworth, and Bonnie Prince Charlie, and, set in a lovely flower garden, *Queen Mary's House*. It was there Mary of Scotland lay ill after riding to visit Bothwell at Hermitage Castle. This 13th-century edifice, one of the oldest baronial buildings in Scotland, is beyond Hawick, about 12 miles west of Jedburgh. Its history of violence is almost as formidable as its age. And Hawick itself represents the modern border country. It is now the center of the area's thriving woolen industry.

Northeast of Jedburgh is **Kelso**, with a large town-square which makes it look almost French. There, too, stand the remains of an Abbey which was probably the largest in Scotland. In 1715 the "Old Pretender," James Stewart, was proclaimed James VIII in Kelso's market place. And here, 30 years later, his son, Charles, brought his troops on their way to invade England.

A few miles west and you will be in the heart of the "Scott country," the lowlands which are the setting for the famous romantic novels. Scott himself lies buried at *Dryburgh Abbey*, a Gothic ruin surrounded by ancient, gnarled yews and Cedars of Lebanon

Bagpipes still wail and the kilt is regulation in Edinburgh Castle

planted there by returning crusaders in the Middle Ages. Seven miles away, at Galashiels, beside the River Tweed, is the novelist's home, *Abbotsford*. Though built in the early 19th century, it is turreted, with colonnades and mammoth rows of chimneys. The mansion is full of mementoes of Scott and his own collection of historical relics.

Sir Walter was not the border country's only author, however. **Peebles**, a woolmill town and fishing resort, was the home of John Buchan and Robert L. Stevenson. R.L.S. drew heavily from the colorful countryside in "Kidnapped." Prosperous, quiet Peebles is now known for its mills, trout, and writers, but it was once the site of the worst of the border atrocities; they still tell you of the football game played with the head of an English warrior.

THE LOWLANDS

The busy, heavily populated lowlands are dominated by the two great Scottish cities, Edinburgh, the capital, and Glasgow. Edinburgh—the "Auld Reekie"—is among the most romantic and interesting cities of northern Europe, proud, strikingly handsome, and ancient. It's a gray city, gold-flecked, and banded with green. Gray is the color of the buildings—old and elegant and angular—and often of the sky. A green park runs between the castle hill and Princes Street, surely one of Europe's most impressive and lovely city thoroughfares. From its windows and doorways come glints of gold, lamplight and the warmth of open fireplaces. Though Edinburgh can be warm and sunny, it comes into its own, somehow, on a wintry day when the street-lights make weird shadows on the buildings and cast reflections on the wet bricks or cobbles of the streets. Then nothing is more pleasant than taking tea (with buttered scones and proper Scottish shortbread, of course) in a little shop on Princes Street while the cars and fantastic double-decked buses hurry by outside.

Edinburgh: castle, galleries, the monument, and Princes Street

Princes Street divides the old city from the new. The "newer" Edinburgh—mainly 18th century—has wide, straight streets, luxury shops, fine restaurants, and all the advantages of a modern city. Steep, narrow lanes, buildings of every shape and condition, tiny squares, and rows of minute shops make up the "old city" which clambers up the side of the hill dominated by the castle. The walk up is an adventure (though not for the easily winded!) and the view from the castle, whether you walk or ride there, is superb. To the north you can see over the Firth of Forth to Fifeshire, and to the northwest, dimly in the distance, you can spot the Highlands.

To walk the *Royal Mile* (Lawnmarket, St. Giles', Canongate), is to stroll through a medieval city. The ancient fortress castle, at the top, has been used as palace and prison, its position at the edge of a precipice making it easy to defend. Even today you'll hear the skirling of the pipes and the tramp of marching feet, for the castle is still the headquarters for kilted Scottish regiments. Within the walls is *St. Margaret's Chapel*, a tiny Norman church founded in 1072 by Queen Margaret, the daughter-in-law of King Duncan, Macbeth's victim. The castle's *Crown Room* houses the Scottish Regalia, older than the Crown Jewels in the Tower of London. (Parliament destroyed most of the English Royal Regalia after the execution of Charles I). The modern Scottish National War Memorial is a dignified and effective building, dedicated to the Scots who gave their lives in two World Wars. At the eastern end of the Palace Yard you'll find the *Royal Apartments*, and among the rooms the tiny bed chamber where Mary of Scotland gave birth to a son, destined to be James I of England as well as James VI of Scotland.

The Royal Mile slopes down from the Castle, past lines of ancient houses. Watch for the *St. Giles*, Edinburgh's principal church. It was built between the 14th and 15th centuries, though the four great columns supporting the tower are said to date from the 12th century. John Knox was minister here from 1559 to 1572. (Farther down the Royal Mile, on High Street, you will see his house projecting into the street.) It was here that Jenny Geddes tossed a stool at the head of the Dean when he attempted to read the order of worship instituted by command of Charles I. The place from which she threw the stool is marked by a brass plaque in the floor. There's also a memorial to the Dean, who's listed as the first and last man to read the service in this church!

At the bottom of the Mile is *Holyrood Palace*, the home of Mary of Scotland from 1561-67 and today the principal royal palace in Scotland. It is not an imposing building, but contains a great deal of historical interest—notably the Picture Gallery with Jacob de Wet's 17th-century portraits of over 100 Scottish kings, a collection remarkable at least for its fantasy. Also well worth seeing are Queen Mary's Apartments, Darnley's Apartments, and the State Apartments. At Holyrood in 1745 Bonnie Prince Charlie was proclaimed "Regent of Scotland, England, France and Dominions," a title he did not retain long.

On the slope south of the Royal Mile is the part of old Edinburgh called Greyfriars where you'll find the buildings of the University, one of Britain's top educational centers, the Oxford and Cambridge of Scotland. Along Chambers Street near the quiet old square called Grassmarket (Burns and Wordsworth were among the patrons of the square's White Hart Inn) is the excellent Royal Scottish Museum, one of Britain's finest. Beyond the Greyfriars Churchyard, on George IV Bridge Street, is a curious drinking fountain with a small statue of a dog, "Greyfriars Bobby," who followed his master's coffin to the churchyard and there remained, becoming a local legend, until his own death fourteen years later.

You'll probably want to do most of your roaming in the Old Town, but on the other side of Edinburgh there are also a number of places worth your attention. The *Scottish National Portrait Gallery* and *Museum of Antiquities*, on Queen Street, will give you a fascinating look at Scottish history and make more exciting your trips into the Highlands. The *Robert L. Stevenson Memorial House*, 8 Howard Place, the writer's birthplace, contains a collection of his manuscripts and mementoes. On Princes Street itself, dominated by the Victorian Gothic Scott Monument, are the *Royal Scottish Academy* (annual exhibit, May to August, and special Festival Exhibit, August and September) and the *National Gallery*, both neo-classic buildings of grand proportions. The collection at the Gallery includes some superb paintings owned by the Earl of Ellesmere—four fine Titians, a group of works by Raphael, and four Rembrandts, among them a splendid self-portrait.

Climbing the Scott Monument is a tradition for visitors to Edinburgh, and if the weather's clear, you should follow custom. If that, plus the climb to the castle, isn't enough for you, the tallest hill near Edinburgh, Arthur's Seat (so called because of the throne-like formation at the summit) affords a magnificent view of Edinburgh and the coast.

In these times Edinburgh is perhaps best known outside of

Britain for its annual festival. For three weeks in late August and early September the city's concert halls and theaters echo with music and drama. The world's great orchestras, soloists, actors and dancers are invited to perform at the Festival and they, in turn, attract throngs of tourists, students and music-lovers. The Festival is a splendid experience, but only if you plan early and make reservations (for hotels as well as performances) well in advance. Your travel agent or the Festival Association in Edinburgh can provide you with information.

During your stay, you should plan to make an excursion to *Linlithgow Palace*, the stately ruin of the royal palace in which Mary of Scotland was born. It overlooks the blue waters of Linlithgow Loch. Nearby is the magnificent home of the Marquis of Linlithgow, *Hopetoun House*, an enormous 18th-century mansion well furnished with paintings, Chippendale furniture and fine porcelain. (Open May 1-Sept. daily except Thursday and Friday 1:30–5:30.) The Palace and Hopetoun House are both near South Queensferry, where you'll get the best possible view of the famous bridge which spans the Firth of Forth.

Eight miles south of Edinburgh are *Rosslyn* (or *Roslin*) *Castle and Chapel*. The chapel is the most ornate piece of Gothic architecture in Britain, a startling example of stone carving from its intricate columns to the flower- and star-covered vaulting. The Castle, much of it carved out of rock (note the kitchens and dungeons) dates from the early 14th century and was partially destroyed in the 16th.

Glasgow, the smoking industrial center of the Lowlands, has little of Edinburgh's charm or historical fascination, but it is a lively city of over a million people, the home of the shipyards that built the great Cunard liners and of several famous chemical and engineering plants. In Glasgow's factories and "The Gorbals," probably the worst slum district in Britain, you'll find the best and worst results of the industrial revolution.

The temper of the city is echoed in its accent—Scots, but with a harsh edge sharpening the gentler burr of Edinburgh and the Highlands. It's not a tourist spot, but if you are curious and venturesome, you will find that a tough sort of good spirits makes the dark streets of this unique city far from depressing. And there is a striking medieval (mostly 13th-century) Cathedral and an important University dating from 1451. The *Art Gallery and Museum* in Kelvingrove Park contains an unusually rich collection of important European paintings.

The western portion of the Lowlands south of Glasgow—sometimes called "Galloway"—is, in fact, relatively high, hilly land. Lying west of the major road-system, it is quiet and open, a popular vacation area. It's also the Burns country. The poet was born near the town of **Ayr** and died in **Dumfries**. The charm and humor of Burns' verse, the most Scottish of all poetry, reflect the mood and

Glamis Castle, a setting for Macbeth

manners of these western hills and villages. You can see his birthplace, a simple thatched cottage built by his father, and the *Tam O'Shanter Inn*, now a Burns museum. Near Ayr there are several famous golf courses, most notably *Turnberry*, and not far away is *Culzean Castle*, with the apartments presented to Eisenhower after the war as his permanent Scottish home. There are also several seaside resorts near Ayr, and from Ardrossan you can take a boat to the tiny *Isle of Arran*, where vacationers bent on tramping the hills or enjoying water sports mingle with the islanders who for centuries have eked a living from the sparse land of their rocky home.

Burns spend his last years in *Dumfries*, and on the lane now called Burns Street you'll find his house. His tomb, somewhat inappropriately in the shape of a Greek temple, is in *St. Michael's Church*. Dumfries, along the lovely River Nith, is also a fine center for trips into the lowlands—to some of the many beautiful lochs and to the braes of Maxwelltown, the "bonny braes" of "Annie Laurie." You should also see at least a few of the splendid medieval buildings scattered among the hills of Galloway—formidable and grim *Threave Castle*, once the citadel of the Douglases who controlled much of the Western lowlands during the Middle Ages, for example, and the gentler, charming *Sweetheart Abbey*.

Across the Firth of Forth from Edinburgh, in the county of Fife, is the ancient town **Dunfermline**, which preceded Edinburgh as capital of Scotland. Andrew Carnegie was born here, and the city has benefited greatly from his generosity. Perhaps most appealing is the lovely park, Carnegie's gift to the people of Dunfermline so that their children would not be forced, as he had been, to stand outside the iron fences looking at gardens which they were forbidden to enter.

To the west is **Stirling**, near the famous battleground Bannockburn. The ancient castle, high on a mammoth, sheer-faced rock, guarded the "gateway to the Highlands." Soldiers who, but for their modern weapons, might be the kilted troops of a Scottish king, still

Home of Sir Walter Scott, Roxburyshire

hold the castle, for it is the headquarters of the Argyle and Sutherland Highlanders, one of Britain's most famous regiments. Below, in a meadow dotted with grazing sheep, you'll be able to spot the mounds and patterns of rocks which mark an old jousting ground, once the site of great knightly tournaments. And beyond, one of the longest stretches of straight road in Britain leads into the Highlands.

This region, called the *Trossachs*, is the country of Scott's *Lady of the Lake* and *Rob Roy*, and here you'll find *Loch Lomond*, the largest lake in Britain and one of the loveliest. There are several villages (and excellent hotels) along its banks, and you can take a steamer trip from one end to the other. But don't neglect the other lakes nearby: *Loch Katrine*, *Loch Achray*, and *Loch Vennachar*.

St. Andrews, an old gray town of ancient houses and monastic ruins on the east shore of Fifeshire, will attract all golf-players because of its famous club, the "Royal and Ancient." However, St. Andrews is also a lovely town in its own right, and seat of an ancient university. It is often called "the Oxford of Scotland," and its students are Britain's liveliest and most prone to extravagant undergraduate shenanigans. A little north is **Leuchars**, a village celebrated for its church, a part of which is splendid 12th-century Romanesque. You'll know already the cakes, marmalade and linen of **Dundee**, across the River Tay from Leuchars. The countryside here is the home of the characters made familiar by Sir James M. Barrie, whose gently written plays brought a deal of Scottish common sense to London and New York.

North of Dundee, you should visit *Glamis Castle* in Angus. Duncan is supposed to have been murdered by Macbeth in this turreted medieval castle (remodelled in the French-château style in the 17th century). Glamis has a less violent recent history, for it was here that the Queen Mother spent her childhood. (Open May-September, Wednesday and Thursday 2-5:30, also Sunday in July, August, September 2-5:30.)

What to See in Scotland and Wales

Upriver from Dundee is the ancient town of Perth, capital of Scotland until the 15th century, and now a factory town. It is another of the gateways to the Highlands. The building to look for here is the well-restored *Church of St. John*, where John Knox preached in 1559. The famous golf course *Gleneagles* is a few miles southwest of Perth. Another sport of sorts, well practiced at the Gleneagles' ball room, is traditional Scottish dancing—foursome and eightsome reels which literally make the specially sprung floor bounce. And if you don't do the dances, you'll still enjoy dinner and watching.

THE HIGHLANDS

The only sizeable city in the whole area loosely called the Highlands is **Aberdeen**, third largest in Scotland. It is a solid, cold, middle-class city built almost entirely of light gray granite. It lies between the mouths of the Don and Dee Rivers, and its fine sand beaches make it a popular resort despite the chilly North Sea winds that come blowing across it. The *Fish Market*, down at the harbor, is the largest in the country. You'll also want to visit *Marischal College*, with its intricately carved façade, and the *Cathedral of St. Machar*, dating from the 14th century, the only ancient granite Cathedral in Britain.

One popular approach to the Highlands is from Aberdeen along the Dee River. You'll quickly see why it's called the "postcard route." The first stop along your way is *Banchory* and *Crathes Castle*, a fine early Jacobean building whose gardens are famous. (Open May–September, daily 2–7, and Wed. and Sun., 2–7 in April and Oct.) Next is **Aboyne,** a very popular summer resort where the Highland Gathering, a fashion-

Loch an Eileen, near Inverness

able event, is held in September. Not far from the town is *Craigievar Castle*, with a fortified tower dating from the late 16th century. And a mile from here is *Macbeth's Cairn*, where legend says Macduff put an end to Macbeth's blood-stained career.

Upriver from Aboyne is the fishing resort Ballater, beautifully set at the foot of the Grampian mountain range. Eight miles beyond is the royal Scottish residence, *Balmoral Castle*, which Victoria loved to visit in her old age, and which still is often occupied by the royal family. (Public admitted to the grounds only when the court is not in residence.)

Braemar, in a lovely valley, is a famous holiday resort and also is a good center from which to make excursions into the neighboring mountains—Lochnagar (3786 ft.), Ben Macdhuie (4296 ft.), and other peaks of the Cairngorm range. The *Braemar Gathering* is the chief social event of the Highland Season. It takes place in early September and usually is attended by the Queen.

To the south, through magnificent mountain passes, is *Blair Atholl*, another attractive holiday center from which you can explore the Perthshire Highlands. Don't miss a visit to *Blair Castle*, a storybook medieval building in the Scottish baronial style. (Open April Sun. and Mon., May 1-Oct. 15 daily: weekdays 10-6, Sun. 2-6.) The neighboring town, *Pitlochry*, has a well-attended theater festival every summer. Directly to the west are a number of fine mountain lakes and passes: the Pass of Killiecrankie, Loch Tummel, Loch Rannoch, Loch Ericht. This is an area in which you can enjoy nature without foregoing any comforts, for everywhere you'll find excellent hotels and all the facilities of fine resort centers.

A good "headquarters" for touring the western Highlands and the Western Isles is **Oban,** a small but bustling port town. Somewhat southeast is Inveraray, ancient and picturesque, dominated by a handsome 18th-century castle. (Open April-June 24, daily except Friday, July-Oct. 3, daily 10-12:30 and 2-6, Sun. 2-6.)

From Oban you can wander inland to *Loch Awe*; or go by boat to the mountainous island of *Mull* (chief town Tobermory), to the tiny uninhabited island *Staffa* with its remarkable caves; the most famous, Fingal's Cave, inspired Mendelssohn's overture. Especially interesting is the little island *Iona*, the first Christian settlement in Scotland, where there is a monastery established by St. Columba, who came from Ireland in 563. The Cathedral is particularly worth seeing. Many of the ancient Scottish kings were buried on Iona, among them both Macbeth and his victim, Duncan.

North of Oban, near the town of Ballachulish, is **Glencoe,** the famous "Glen of Weeping," scene of a brutal massacre in 1692. Brutality seems almost incredible in the magnificent scenery of this pass through superb mountains.

North of Ballachulish lies what is perhaps the most beautiful part of the Highlands, the *Caledonian Canal*, a system of interlocked

Most famous of the Scottish lakes, Loch Lomond

lakes leading from Fort William to Inverness. You can travel the Canal by boat or follow its banks in your car. Fort William itself is a popular holiday resort, and also the best place from which to ascend *Ben Nevis* (4406 ft.), Britain's highest peak. Fort Augustus is a comfortable stopping-off place, and it's near *Loch Ness*, in whose depths—according to those who've been about for his rare trips to the surface—lives the famous Loch Ness monster. He's not likely to put in an appearance for you, but the Loch itself is well worth your visit. Midway up the Loch, at Drumnadrochit, you will want to see the romantic ruins of *Urquhart Castle*.

At the north end of the Canal is that pleasant town *Inverness*, "capital of the Highlands," ancient in its history but thoroughly modern in spirit. There is an interesting museum here, with Jacobean relics. Near the town is the impressive battlefield of *Culloden*, where stones engraved with the names of famous clans mark the graves of the Highlanders killed in 1746 in Bonnie Prince Charlie's last battle.

The *Hebrides*, those wild Scottish islands which have fascinated travelers in search of out-of-the-way sights and adventures even before Dr. Johnson and Boswell visited them in the 18th century, can be reached either from *Mallaig*, or *Kyle of Lochalsh*. In the Inner Hebrides you'll come upon such flatly named little islands as Muck, Eigg and Rum before you reach the **Isle of Skye**, the largest and most famous—both because of its association with Prince Charlie and Flora MacDonald (who took him here disguised as Betty Burke after the Culloden defeat), and because of its rugged mountain scenery.

The **Outer Hebrides**, reached from the same inland ports, are wild, melancholy islands, populated mostly by crofters and fishermen who generally speak only Gaelic. In contrast with the rest of Scotland, the home of "the kirk," the people here are Roman Catholic and they have many close, ancient associations with the Gaelic Irish. The largest island is Lewis, and its southern extension, Harris. Stornoway is the only real town in the island group whose attractions are wild scenery, boating and fine fishing. The islands do have one more distinction. They produce some of the finest tweeds made.

WALES

You will quickly feel that Wales (a principality, by the way) is a different country from England. And you will be right: it is different. It has a different racial origin, a different language, different culture, different history—and a different look. Like Cornwall, Wales harbors the last authentic Celtic remnants of ancient Britain. It has been said that Britain is most truly British in Wales; because it was to the mountain retreats of Wales that the original inhabitants of Britain fled and succeeded in holding fast to their own language and way of life, while the rest of Britain was assimilating the Romans, Angles, Saxons, Danes, and Normans. Though the Celts were driven back and finally brought under the English yoke, they were never assimilated. The Welsh have endured in spite of so many defeats because, though they accepted the political sovereignty of the English (much sooner than the Scots), they never gave up any of their cultural independence. Their nationalist movement is not pugnacious; their values tend to be spiritual rather than material ones. They are a people nourished on legends, the supernatural, and song; they adore music and poetry. They have suffered tremendously, are mostly poor, yet show a kind of simple cheerfulness and amiability that makes one respect them. Someone (an Englishman) has said that the difference between English and Welsh towns at the border is that in the Welsh towns the people smile.

Wales itself falls naturally into two divisions: north and south. If you have only a short amount of time, you must choose the North, because it is far more beautiful and hardly spoiled at all by the taint of industrialization. These peaceful rural counties of the north (Flintshire, Caernarvonshire, Anglesey, Denbighshire, Merionethshire, and Montgomeryshire) also offer Welsh scenery at its best: the mountains and valleys and waterfalls. Mining, industry, and population are concentrated in the southern counties (Radnorshire, Cardiganshire, Pembrokeshire, Carmarthenshire, Breconshire, and Glamorganshire), and ugliness has found its way here. It hasn't daunted the hardy Welsh, however, and there are still many beautiful places here, especially along the coast. (Monmouthshire is in a curious position, neither quite Welsh or quite English.) We can

What to See in Scotland and Wales

thank Edward I for the great number of fortified castles you see everywhere in Wales. He had to construct them (there are more than a hundred castles remaining in Wales) to keep the unsubmissive Welsh in line. It seems almost accidental that they were also beautiful.

After England, you may find that Wales takes a little while to get used to. Its architecture is simple, the stone generally used for construction is rough and dark gray, giving the country a relatively grim and bleak look. But eventually you will find that look appropriate, and you will learn that it is not stern.

SOUTH WALES

The largest city and capital of Wales is **Cardiff** (Glamorgan), on the river Taff (Welshmen are affectionately called "Taffy"). It is one of Britain's main ports and probably the biggest coal-exporting port in the world. The land just behind it is rich in coal, particularly the Rhondda Valley, and in small, unattractive manufacturing towns. Cardiff is thought of as cosmopolitan, not really Welsh: being a great seaport keeps it constantly in touch with the outside world. On the whole it has the look of a 19th-century city, spacious and dignified, with many attractive areas once you get away from the docks. The civic center in Cathays Park is a garden surrounded by a fine group of modern municipal buildings, including the University College of South Wales and the interesting National Museum of Wales.

Cardiff Castle, in the middle of town near the civic center, is a Norman fortress begun in the 11th century, on the site of a Roman camp. (Open March, April, Oct., weekdays 10 to 12, 2 to 4; May through Sept., 10 to 12, 2 to 8. Sun. 2 to 5.)

While you are here, see the *Cathedral of Llandaff*, on the outskirts of Cardiff. A 12th-century church recently restored after severe

Llangolen's Eisteddfod attracts singers from all over the world

bombing during the last war, it has a startling modern sculpture of *Christ in Majesty* by Epstein.

About five miles from Cardiff is *St. Fagan's Castle*, which houses the unique *Welsh Folk Museum* on extensive grounds where old cottages, farmhouses, and other historical reproductions of ancient Wales have been set up in a lively exhibition.

To the north is *Caerphilly*, famous for cheese and the magnificent medieval ruins of the largest castle in Wales (second only to Windsor in size), which was captured in 1403 by the Welsh hero, Owen Glendower.

The city of Swansea, further westward along the coast, a large industrial port and university center, can be by-passed; but the small *Gower Peninsula*, beyond it, begins a region of delightfully rural scenery and fine bathing. Gower is populated mainly by descendants of the Flemish weavers settled there by Henry VII, and they speak only English, in contrast to their neighbors. There are two ruined castles here, Penrice and Oystermouth, evidence of the fighting that went on in earlier days. *The Mumbles* is the name of the popular resort area on the Gower Peninsula and a good place from which to explore this countryside.

The **Carmarthen Valley**, north of Swansea, is one of the most characteristically Welsh in atmosphere. These are the fertile open hills, most of them slag covered and mine-pitted now, so poignantly pictured in Richard Llewelyn's "How Green Was My Valley." The Towy, a salmon river, flows through the soft dales here, and *Carmarthen* itself, an old market town, has always been the focus of Celtic life. It is the reputed (one of several) birthplace of the Wizard Merlin.

The county of **Pembrokeshire**, the southwest tip of Wales, is sometimes called "Little England beyond Wales." It is a largely non-Welsh-speaking section, since this was another place where Flemish weavers were forcibly settled in the 12th century. The ancient walled town of *Tenby* was turned into an elegant Regency seaside resort in the 18th century: one of the more attractive resorts in the country.

The castle at **Pembroke** is the most impressive ruin in Wales. Henry VII was born here, and it was the scene of intense fighting up to the Civil War.

Milford Haven, once an important seaport and smuggling center because it has the largest natural harbor in Britain, is now a center for the fishing trawler fleet; Lord Nelson's Lady Hamilton lived and is buried here. In the small market town of Haverfordwest on the banks of the Cleddav, there are the 13th-century, fine Church of St. Mary and a Norman castle now prudently put to use as a police station.

Your main target in this area, however, will be **St. David's**, the

What to See in Scotland and Wales

"holy city" of Wales. In this smallest cathedral city in all of Britain, really a tiny village, *St. David's Cathedral* is the finest medieval church in Wales. It has a peculiar situation, set in a large hollow, rather than on the usual high ground, so that you have to descend 39 steps to enter. As you approach it, you can at first see only the top of its tower. The exterior is simple, almost austere, but the interior is a miracle of rich decoration. Bishop Vaughan's chapel has a beautifully carved oak roof.

The inland county of **Breconshire** is noted for its two majestic mountains: the silvery Brecon Beacons and the Black Mountains, now part of a National Park area whose beauty is safeguarded forever. The county town of Brecon, situated at the joining of the Usk and Honddu Rivers, has a 15th-century church of more than usual interest, and should be kept in mind as a good center for boating, mountaineering, fishing, and golfing in this region.

Small **Radnorshire**, created by Henry VIII on the border and largely English-speaking, is the most sparsely populated county, lacking good grazing land or mining possibilities. But the beautiful Wye River flows through its valley and the moorlands of Radnor Forest have attractive scenery. Elan Valley—a man-made chain of lakes which provides Birmingham with water—is lovely but cannot compare to the more dramatic scenery of the north. Radnor is visited mainly by those interested in its excellent spa, *Llandrindod Wells*, which has two rivals in Breconshire, *Builth* and *Llanwrtyd Wells*.

Cardiganshire, usually cited as the "most Welsh" of the counties, where you hear almost nothing but the musical cadences of the Welsh tongue, has an attractive long coastline and a mountainous section in the north. It is a pastoral area of small farms, streams, and valleys. The only important town of any size is **Aberystwyth**, on the coast, the center for mid-Wales, a bathing resort, and the

Tintern Abbey in the half-English, half-Welsh hills of Monmouthshire

104   Britain

oldest university town in Wales. You'll find it a simple, dignified place, with little of the usual British seaside resort tarnish.

If you like waterfalls, go inland to one of the most notable beauty spots in Wales, *Devil's Bridge*, on the Rheidol River, where you can get wonderful views of the Cyfarllwyd and Mynach Falls, a setting of wild torrents, crags, and chasms. "The Bridge of the Evil One" is an ancient structure of stone between two frightening cliffs, supposed to have been built by the devil himself. (Don't confuse it with the 18th-century stone bridge and the modern iron one, which are both above it.)

The county town **Cardigan**, in the southern part on the Teifi River, has the ruins of a medieval castle; still another castle is situated in nearby Cilgerran. On the Teifi here you may still see the traditional tarred-canvas little boat, the "coracle," being used for salmon fishing. This type of fragile boat, so lightweight it can be carried on the back, has been used here for more than a thousand years.

NORTH WALES

This area of spectacular scenery is dominated by *Snowdon*, 3,560 feet, a surprising peak in this part of the world, but there are other good reasons for spending some time here. For one thing, there are excellent beaches all along the coast: Aberdovey, Barmouth, Criccieth, and all the delightful unassuming towns between. Avoid Llandudno and Rhyl: they are attractive but now too popular with hordes of holiday-makers from the north and the Midlands. A peak less overwhelming, but no less legendary, than Snowdon is *Cader Idris* (the legendary chair of the heroic giant bard called Idris), which is easily accessible from Barmouth or Dolgelley, and is worth climbing for the view. This region, combining so conveniently all

Harlech Castle dates from the time of Edward I

What to See in Scotland and Wales 105

the charms of sea and mountain scenery, was chosen by Shelley, Tennyson, Darwin, and Ruskin as an ideal place to work. Both **Dolgelley**, an excellent center for touring, and **Machynlleth**, to the south on the Dovey River, are ancient market towns romantically situated among mountains. The great Welsh hero, Owen Glendower, lived in this part of Wales, and was crowned Prince of Wales and held his Parliament in Machynlleth before starting out on his brave attempt to drive out the English.

Harlech, (celebrated in the stirring song "Men of Harlech" for its gallant refusal to surrender during the War of the Roses), a small Merioneth town on the coast with precipitous streets, has become a symbol of Welsh fortitude. The well-preserved *Harlech Castle*, dramatically set on a high rocky summit, is typical of the fortresses built by Edward I to make his rule stick.

In Portmadoc, stop to visit the odd estate called *Port Meirion*, which is a very lavish model sea village, an artists' colony on elaborate Italianate grounds.

To the west of here is the gorse-covered *Lleyn* (sometimes called Nevin peninsula), where there are golden sandy beaches with excellent swimming at Pwllheli. *Criccieth*, aside from its own charms of lovely panoramas of sea and mountains, is the birthplace of Lloyd George.

The island of **Anglesey**, which juts out to the northwest off Caernarvonshire, was the "Mona" of the Romans, and has a special significance for the Welsh as the "mother" of the Principality, the last refuge of the Druids in ancient times. Like most places in Wales, this lovely island has a legend: it exerts a magnetic force so that anyone who has ever been there must come back again. (This legend is true.) It's rich wheat-growing land, with picturesque windmills and charming unpretentious sandy coves. The first town you come to after crossing the Menai Suspension Bridge, which joins the island to the mainland (an amazing engineering feat for the 19th century), is the one with the longest name in the world, **Llanfairpwllgwyngyllgogerychwyrndrobwllllantysiliogogogoch**. You will always see visitors photographing the unbelievable sign at the railway station. The village people like to say the whole word and know what it means—"The-church-of-St.-Mary-on-the-pool-of-the-white-hazel-by-the-raging-whirlpool-near-the-church-of-St.-Tysilio-of-the-Red-Cave"—but the post office insists on writing it Llanfair P. G.

In the quiet little watering town of Beaumaris you should see the *Edward I Castle*, with its intriguing system of concentric defense: a moat, an outside wall, and an inner wall connecting the towers.

The Marquis of Anglesey's handsome home on the Island, *Plas Newydd*, is late 18th century in the "Gothick" style of James Wyatt. It may be visited freely (and free) but only by writing for an appointment.

On the mainland is *Caernarvon*, which has medieval walls almost intact and *Caernarvon Castle*, the finest of all fortresses erected in Wales by Edward I (after his conquest in 1282) to keep the rebellious Welsh in line. The birth of Edward II took place here, in a political attempt to give the Welsh a king they could accept as their own. Edward I was so anxious to show his child "born on Welsh soil and whose first words would be Welsh" to the Welsh chieftains—who had refused to accept a prince of English birth—that he exposed the baby to them in a sharp wind. The first future Prince of Wales caught a cold of which he almost died.

The inland town of **Beddgelert**, delightfully situated on two rivers at the foot of Snowdon, is bathed in local legends, especially that of the noble hound Gelert after whom it is named. From here you can ascend Snowdon by railroad or by foot. You will be warned, if you are an inexperienced climber, that Snowdon is treacherous. Take the warning seriously. Every summer a number of rash climbers die needlessly on the mountain. The view from Snowdon is so indescribably magnificent on a clear day that you should inquire to make sure the peak is clear of mist before going up.

There are many breath-takingly beautiful passes in the Snowdon range, such as Nant Ffrancon and Llanberis, and right in the midst of these mountains are soft valley towns, the loveliest being the artists' delight, Bettwys-y-Coed, and Capel Curig. The scenery in all of this country is prodigal: even if mountains don't thrill you, there are delightful valleys, unsurpassed fishing, wonderful woods for hiking, and delicate waterfalls.

Bangor, at the mouth of the Menai Straits, has a cathedral, started in the 12th century, then rebuilt many times, and the University of North Wales, with a fine library and museum.

Penrhyn Castle, an estate of over 700 acres outside of Bangor, was built in the mid-19th century of local Mona marble in the Norman style. (Open April, May, Oct., Mon., Wed., Thurs., 2–5, June-Sept., weekdays, 11–6; Sun., July and Aug. only, 2–5.)

The town of **Conway** is a medieval walled city, with a relatively small, but striking castle. The 15-foot wide walls with 21 towers built by Edward I at the same time as the castle, are extraordinarily well preserved, and you can circle the town on them and enjoy fine views from the height.

The mansion *Plas Mawr* (in Conway) is a delightful example of Elizabethan architecture, with many gables and a handsome octagonal tower. (Daily except Sun. 10 to 5:30, winter 10 to 4.)

Four miles south are *Bodnant Gardens*, among the finest in Britain, situated above the Conway River with extraordinary views of the Snowdon range. (April-Oct., daily except Fri., Sun. and Mon. 1:30 to 4:45.)

Rhyl, on the Denbighshire coast, is called the "Welsh Riviera" because of the way the mountains slope right down to the sea. There

Caernarvonshire: Llyn Padarn

are fine 13th-century scenic drives here. Visit *St. Asaph* for its tiny cathedral, the smallest in Great Britain.

A town of unusual charm and interest in Denbighshire is **Llangollen**, beside the River Dee and surrounded by wooded hills. The annual International Eisteddfod in which more than 25 countries vie with each other in folk singing and dancing, takes place here every July.

The house called *Plas Newydd* was the home in the late 18th century of Lady Eleanor Butler and the Hon. Sarah Ponsonby, two romantic and eccentric young women who fled here from their home in Ireland and came to be known as the "Ladies of Llangollen." They were determined to be intellectual and never marry, and they kept busy knitting blue stockings (creating a new English expression). They were visited by notable people such as Wellington, De Quincey, Scott, and Wordsworth, all of whom brought gifts to add to their collection. (By written appointment only.)

Outside the town is *Valle Crucis Abbey*, interesting and substantial ruins of a 13th-century Cistercian abbey. Another nearby place of interest is Bryn-Eglwys, whose chapel belonged to the Yale family and is now dedicated to Elihu Yale, founder of Yale University.

In nearby Wrexham, don't miss *Chirk Castle*, which has been lived in continuously since the year 1310. It has interesting furniture and decorations. (Open May-Sept., Tues., Thurs., Sat., Sun. 2 to 5.)

Two inland lakes, *Bala*, in Merionethshire, and *Vyrnwy*, in Montgomeryshire, make excellent stopping-off places for relaxation from sightseeing. They have good accommodations, pleasant scenery, fishing, walking, and easy mountain climbing.

Not far from Vyrnwy, outside the town of Welshpool, is *Powis Castle*, a reconstructed medieval building of red sandstone, with splendid interiors and unique hanging gardens. (Castle and gardens open June-Sept., daily except Mon. and Tues., 2–6.)

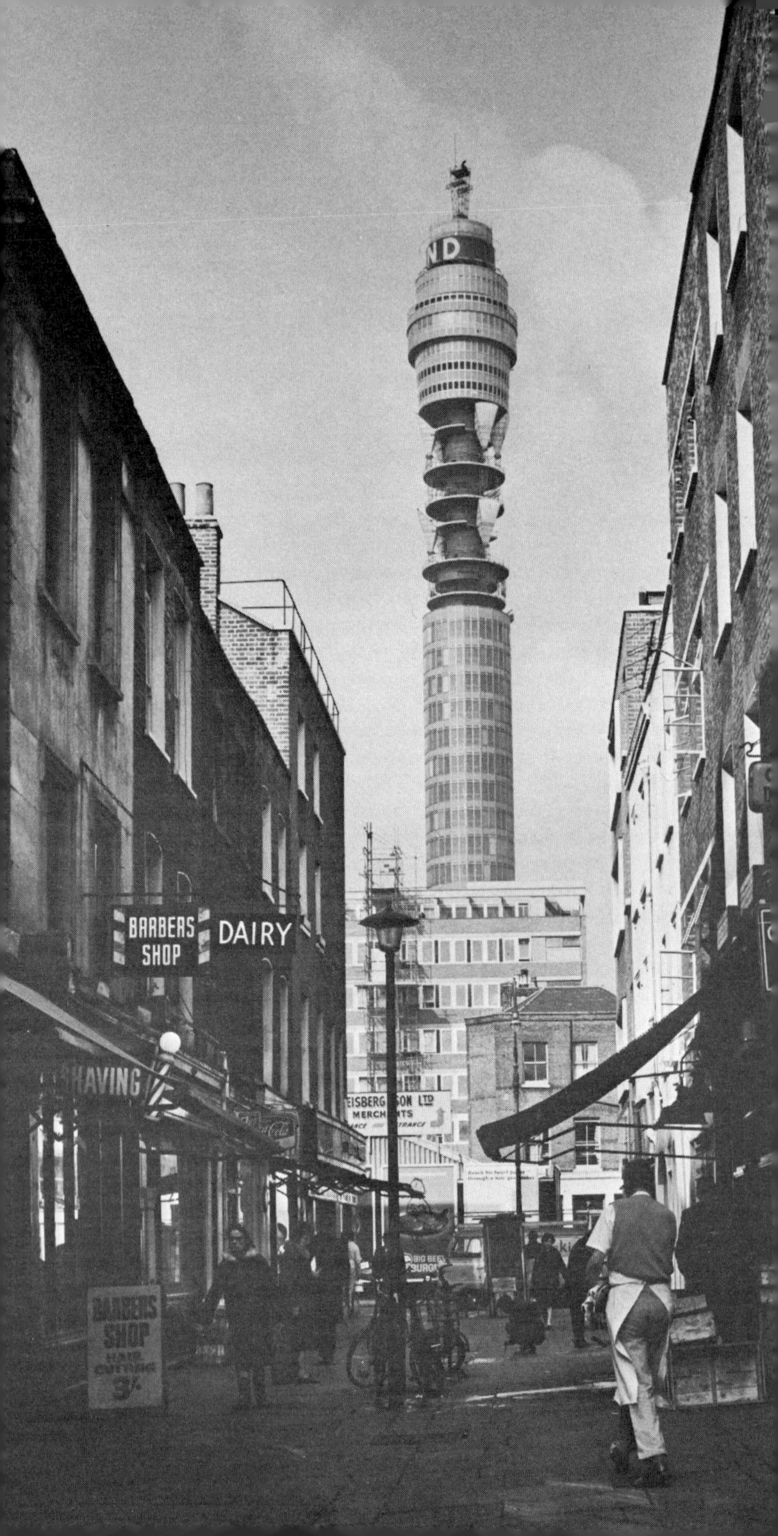
BARBERS SHOP
DAIRY
SHAVING
BARBERS SHOP
MERCHANTS

CHAPTER 6

FACT FINDER

The countryside of Great Britain is dotted with thousands of hotels, ranging from mammoth, elegant establishments with private golf courses, to tiny inns with five or six rooms which have been serving travelers for hundreds of years. Inns, as a matter of fact, are one of the most delightful phenomena of Britain and their dining rooms often are among the country's best restaurants.

In the list below, hotels are grouped according to price and, within these price categories, alphabetically. At de luxe hotels, marked by three stars (***) you can expect to pay upward from 5 pounds ($12.25) for a single room to 9 pounds ($22.05) for a double room with private bath. Hotels with 2 stars (**) will run upward from 4 pounds ($9.80) for a single room to 7 pounds ($17.15) for a double with bath. Hotels marked by one star (*) are more inexpensive, and can start at 2.50 pounds ($6.13) and go up to about 5 pounds ($12.25) for a double. Of course, there is a considerable range of prices within the categories and it always is wise to confirm the actual prices you will pay when you make your reservations or check into your hotel.

Ordinarily, the room charges in British hotels include breakfast but do not include service. Though some hotels in London have adopted the continental system of adding automatically a service charge, this is not true at most hotels and you will be expected to tip. The symbol (T) after the name of a hotel means that it has no liquor license. The symbol (LC) indicates a licensed club on the premises. Private baths are available at many hotels but they are by no means the rule; therefore the number of private baths at each hotel is listed after the number of rooms (as: "35 rooms, 15 p.b.").

The restaurants mentioned in the list are not categorized by price.

new Post Office Tower looms over old London

Unless some special note is given that the restaurant is expensive or particularly cheap, you may assume that the tariff will be somewhere in the middle range—between, say, £1.50 and £2 ($3.60 and $4.80). The adage, which holds true so often on the Continent, that a hotel dining room is serviceable but definitely unexciting, loses its meaning in Great Britain. Hotels, especially the country inns, are among the best places to eat. In fact, many of the inns, though they do have some overnight accommodations, are much more famous for their splendid cuisine—and you have every reason to expect fine cooking as well as charming atmosphere at a good inn. Therefore, when looking for restaurants in the Fact Finder, remember to glance at the hotel listings as well as the establishments specifically noted under "Restaurants."

ENGLAND

Abingdon (pop. 18,600)
HOTEL: *Crown and Thistle.* 26 rooms.
Alfriston (pop. 600)
HOTELS: **Deans Place.* (LC) 42 rooms, 25 p.b. *Star Inn.* 34 rooms. 15th century inn, plain English food.
Alton (pop. 11,000) (near Chawton, Jane Austen's house)
HOTEL: *Swan.* 17 rooms, 3 p.b. Good restaurant.
Ambleside (pop. 2,500) on Lake Windermere.
HOTELS: *Skelwith Bridge.* 22 rooms, 16 p.b. *Salutation.* 31 rooms, 2 p.b.
RESTAURANT: *Dungeon Ghyll Old Hotel* (in Great Langdale). Hearty food well cooked, cheap.
Amersham (pop. 14,600)
HOTEL: *Crown.* 15 rooms. Old inn, meals above average.
Amesbury (pop. 5,600)
HOTEL: *George.* 22 rooms, 1 p.b. Garden restaurant. *Antrobus Arms.* 20 rooms, 5 p.b.
Ampthill (pop. 4,300)
HOTEL: *White Hart.* 7 rooms. Good variety of food, moderate prices.

Arundel (pop. 3,000)
HOTEL: **Norfolk Arms.* 18 rooms, 10 p.b. Interesting old building.
RESTAURANTS: *Maltravers.* Attractive interior, fashionable clientele. *Black Rabbit Inn* (at Crossbush). Well-cooked plain food, reasonable. *Camelia* (at Crossbush). Good food.
Ascot (pop. 7,200)
HOTELS: **Berystede.* 92 rooms, 92 p.b. *Royal Foresters.* 10 rooms. (Book well ahead for Royal Ascot week.)
Aston Clinton (pop. 2,800)
HOTEL: *The Bell.* 4 rooms. Good French food and wines.
Aylesbury (pop. 32,500)
HOTEL: *Ye Old Bull's Head.* 32 rooms, 3 p.b. *King's Head.* 15 rooms.
RESTAURANT: *The Crown.* Lunches only, dinner Saturday. Good grills at inexpensive prices.
Bagshot (pop. 3,500)
HOTEL: *Cricketers'.* 15 rooms, 1 p.b. Excellent food and wine list.
Bamburgh (pop. 600)
HOTELS: **Lord Crewe Arms.* 17 rooms, 12 p.b. Reliable dining room, moderately expensive. *Victoria.* 30 rooms.
Banbury (pop. 29,000)
HOTELS: **Whately Hall.* 78 rooms, 50 p.b. Well-known luxury hotel, excellent food. *The Green Man,* 10 miles away at Brackley Hatch, has an excellent restaurant.
Barnstaple (pop. 16,000)
HOTELS: *Imperial.* 54 rooms, 41 p.b. *Royal and Fortescue,* 38 rooms, 6

p.b. Near Bideford, nine miles south of Barnstaple, is the old *Portledge Hotel,* 35 rooms, 19 p.b., at Fairy Cross, and the ancient *Hoops Inn,* 16 rooms, at Horns Cross, both fine inns.

Bath (pop. 84,500)

HOTELS: **Francis.* 84 rooms, 26 p.b. Splendid restaurant. **Lansdown Grove,* 50 rooms, 13 p.b. **Royal York.* 60 rooms, 17 p.b. *Cleveland.* 60 rooms, 12 p.b.

RESTAURANTS: *The Hole in the Wall,* 16–17 George St. Unusual meals, well cooked: a trifle arty.

Battle (pop. 4,300)

HOTEL: **Beauport Park.* (LC) 20 rooms, 18 p.b.

Bedford (pop. 73,000)

HOTELS: ***County.* 80 rooms, 70 p.b. **Swan.* 71 rooms, 41 p.b.

Berwick-upon-Tweed (pop. 12,700)

HOTEL: **King's Arms.* 30 rooms, 4 p.b.

Bexhill-on-Sea (pop. 31,200)

HOTEL: **Granville.* 53 rooms, 2 p.b.

Birmingham (pop. 1,000,000)

HOTELS: ***Albany,* Smallbrook. 264 rooms, 254 p.b. New, first-class. Good restaurant. ***Midland,* New St. 122 rooms, 47 p.b. ***Royal Angus.* 140 rooms, 140 p.b. **Imperial,* Temple St. 78 rooms.

RESTAURANT: *Savoy,* Hill Street. *La Cappanna,* Hurst Street. *Lambert Court.* First class, with spacious grounds. French dishes. Soho atmosphere. *Plough and Harrow.* Modern, generally good food. Fine wine list. *Outrigger.* Mostly fish and seafood.

Blackpool (pop. 147,000)

HOTELS: ***Imperial,* North Promenade. 158 rooms, 98 p.b. **Savoy.* 144 rooms, 30 p.b. **Clifton,* Talbot Sq. 91 rooms, 36 p.b.

RESTAURANTS: *Stuart Hotel,* Clifton Drive. Friendly atmosphere, goodish food. *Lobster Pot,* 35 Market St.

Fact Finder 111

Good fish at reasonable prices.

Bodinnick (pop. 1,400)

HOTEL: **Old Ferry Inn.* 11 rooms, 3 p.b. Beautiful location, good food.

Bognor Regis (pop. 34,000)

HOTEL: **Royal Norfolk.* 56 rooms, 41 p.b.

Borrowdale (pop. 630)

HOTELS: **Lodore Swiss.* 73 rooms, 64 p.b. Attractive location, fine Swiss cuisine. *Borrowdale.* 30 rooms, 7 p.b.

Boston (pop. 24,000)

HOTEL: **New England.* 11 rooms, 5 p.b.

Bournemouth (pop. 154,000)

HOTELS: ***Palace Court,* Westover Road. 120 rooms all with p.b. ***Royal Bath,* Bath Road. 131 rooms, 131 p.b.

RESTAURANTS: *Czech Restaurant,* 728 Christchurch Rd., Bascombe. Pleasant Middle European cooking, inexpensive. *Continental,* Holdenhurst Rd. *London Steak House,* 19-21 Bourne Ave. Steaks, fish, good wines. *Royal Bath Hotel.* Restaurant and Buttery, fine French food, not cheap.

Bourton-on-the-Water (pop. 2,000)

HOTEL: *Old New Inn.* 25 rooms, 1 p.b. Popular Cotswolds inn.

Bovey Tracey (pop. 3,000)

HOTELS: **Edgemoor.* 23 rooms, 3 p.b. Interesting meals.

Bradford (pop. 292,500) Near *Haworth,* Bronte home.

HOTEL: **Midland.* 71 rooms, 23 p.b.

Bridport (pop. 6,300)

HOTEL: *Greyhound.* 20 rooms. Old inn, good food, moderate prices.

Brighton and Hove (pop. 235,400)

HOTELS: ***Dudley,* Landsdown, Hove. 75 rooms, 70 p.b. **Metropole,* King's Rd., 275 rooms, 275 p.b. **Queen's,* King's Rd., 87 rooms, 30 p.b.

RESTAURANTS: *English's Oyster Bar,*

East St. Fish specialties, medium prices. *Pump House*, 46 Market St. Elegant house in old Brighton. A la carte, expensive. *Queen's Hotel.* Good English cooking. *Wheeler's Sheridan Tavern*, 83 West Street. Fish generally. Lobster bisque a specialty.

Bristol (pop. 444,000)
HOTELS: ****Grand,* Broad St. 197 rooms, 106 p.b. ****Grand Spa,* Clifton. 66 rooms, 39 p.b. ***Royal,* College. 134 rooms, 58 p.b. Good hotel cooking.
RESTAURANTS: *Harvey's,* 12 Denmark St. *Ox on the Roof.* Small good bistro.

Brixham (pop. 11,300)
HOTELS: ***Northcliffe.* 64 rooms, 12 p.b. **Quayside,* on the Bay. 32 rooms, 1 p.b.

Broadstairs (pop. 19,000)
HOTELS: **Castle Keep,* in Kingsgate. 20 rooms, 15 p.b. **Royal Albion,* 29 rooms.
RESTAURANT: *Marchesi Brothers.* good food, Italian wines.

Broadway (pop. 2,700)
HOTELS: ****Lygon Arms.* 54 rooms, 32 p.b. Unusually fine food. ***Swan,* 7 rooms.

Brockenhurst (pop. 2,661)
HOTEL: ****Carey's Manor.* 56 rooms, 45 p.b. In a lovely part of the country.

Burford (pop. 1,450)
HOTELS: ***Lamb Inn.* 14 rooms, 4 p.b. Comfortable; good food. **Cotswold Gateway.* 13 rooms. 2 p.b. 16th-century inn, memorable.

At Newbridge is *The Rose Revived,* an ancient inn as lovely and unusual as its name—on the bank of a river beside the "new" (extremely old) bridge; the food is as good as the setting.

Bury St. Edmunds (pop. 26,000)

HOTELS: ***Angel.* 50 rooms, 13 p.b. *The Bull Inn,* at Barton Mills, eleven miles northwest of Bury. 15 rooms, 6 p.b. Charming and the restaurant is famous—roast Norfolk duck, pheasant in season.

Buxton (pop. 20,000)
HOTELS: ***Palace.* 139 rooms, 66 p.b. ***St. Ann's.* 55 rooms, 12 p.b.

Cambridge (pop. 98,000)
HOTELS: ***Garden House.* 58 rooms, 15 p.b. ***University Arms.* 126 rooms, 80 p.b. **Blue Boar,* 47 rooms, 7 p.b.
RESTAURANTS: *Bistro Italo,* 21 Northampton St. *Arts Theatre,* 6 St. Edward's Passage. Good menu, moderate prices. *Miller's Wine Parlour,* King's Parade. Fairly ambitious food, wines featured, moderately expensive. *Le Jardin.* Small, simple, but excellent food. Owner cooks for you.

Canterbury (pop. 32,000)
HOTELS: ***Slatter's.* 30 rooms, 23 p.b. ***Chaucer.* 47 rooms, 29 p.b. **Abbots Barton.* 33 rooms, 18 p.b.
RESTAURANT: Near Canterbury (at Bridge) is *The White Horse,* a fine 16th-century inn.

Carlisle (pop. 71,000)
HOTELS: ***County.* 68 rooms, 14 p.b. ***Crown and Mitre.* 76 rooms, 49 p.b.

Chagford (pop. 1800)
HOTELS: ***Easton Court.* 15 rooms, 1 p.b. Splendid restaurant. **Moorlands.* 24 rooms, 6 p.b. **Great Tree.* 17 rooms, 9 p.b. An old hunting lodge.

Cheddar (pop. 2,600)
HOTEL: **Cliff.* 24 rooms.

Cheltenham (pop. 76,000)
HOTELS: ****Carlton.* 49 rooms, 49 p.b. ***Plough,* High St. 64 rooms, HOTELS: ***Belle Vue.* 55 rooms, 5 p.b. ***Plough,* High St. 64 rooms, 7 p.b. ***Queen's,* Promenade. 70 rooms, 21 p.b. Elegant dining room.
RESTAURANTS: *The Black Tulip.* Regency House on the Promenade.

Good food. Exciting dessert cart. Inexpensive.
Chester (pop. 57,000)
HOTELS: ***Grosvenor.** 100 rooms, 100 p.b. **Blossoms.* 109 rooms, 51 p.b. Exceptionally good food, not cheap.
RESTAURANT: *Bolland's Buttery*, Eastgate Row. Good standard of straightforward food, not expensive.
Chesterfield (pop. 68,000)
HOTEL: **Station.* 60 rooms, 20 p.b.
Chichester (pop. 20,000)
HOTELS: ***Chichester Motel.* 34 rooms, 34 p.b. **Ship.* 30 rooms, 12 p.b.
RESTAURANTS: *Old Cross Inn.* The eating utensils are luxurious; the food, passable.
Chiddingfold (pop. 2,200)
HOTEL: **Crown Inn.* 7 rooms, 4 p.b. Fine restaurant (trout, good cheeses, extensive wine list).
Chipping Camden (pop. 2,000)
HOTEL: *Cotswold House.* 18 rooms, 3 p.b. *Noel Arms*, 15 rooms, 4 p.b.
Chipping Norton (pop. 4,700)
HOTEL: **White Hart.* 13 rooms.
Chipping Sodbury (pop. 1,100)
HOTEL: *°Portcullis,* 5 rooms.
Church Stretton (pop. 2,700)
HOTEL: *Longmynd.* 60 rooms, 17 p.b.
Cirencester (pop. 11,700)
HOTELS: **King's Head.* 52 rooms, 25 p.b. **Stratton House.* 32 rooms, 17 p.b. *Crown Hotel.* 15 rooms. Fine restaurant.
Clevedon (pop. 14,300)
HOTEL: **Walton Park.* 38 rooms, 7 p.b.
Clovelly (pop. 445)
HOTEL: *New Inn.* 20 rooms. Excellent restaurant with particularly fine table wines.
Colchester (pop. 69,000)
HOTELS: **George.* 39 rooms, 12 p.b. **Red Lion.* 40 rooms, 4 p.b. Roast meats are excellent, inexpensive.
Coventry (pop. 335,000)
HOTELS: ***Leofric.* 97 rooms, 70 p.b. New commercial hotel. Good food, but not cheap. **Allesley.* 27 rooms, 13 showers.
Cromer (pop. 5,000)
HOTELS: **Hotel de Paris.* 59 rooms, 14 p.b. The *Overstrand Court,* in Overstrand, offers excellent seafood and fresh, local berries in season.
Dartmouth (pop. 6,000)
HOTELS: *Raleigh.* 36 rooms. Overlooks the sea. *Victoria,* 8 rooms. Very good fish.
Derby (pop. 217,000)
HOTEL: **Midland.* 62 rooms, 14 p.b.
RESTAURANT: *Golden Pheasant,* English and Continental cuisine, reasonable prices.
Doncaster (pop. 82,000)
HOTELS: **Danum.* 71 rooms, 13 p.b. Good careful meals, inexpensive. **Punch's.* 26 rooms, 15 p.b. Up-to-date modern hotel, good Continental meals.
Dorking (pop. 22,000)
HOTEL: **White Horse.* 37 rooms, 36 p.b.
Dovedale
HOTEL: **Izaak Walton.* 26 rooms, 13 p.b. Attractive location, fishing center. Excellent home cooking.
Dover (pop. 35,250)
HOTELS: **White Cliffs.* 75 rooms, 21 p.b.
RESTAURANT: *Britannia,* Townwall St.
Droitwich (pop. 13,000)
HOTELS: **Raven.* 60 rooms, 30 p.b. **Worcestershire.* 100 rooms, 65 p.b.
Durham (pop. 23,000)
HOTEL: **Royal County.* 58 rooms, 4 p.b. *Three Tuns,* 16 rooms.
Eastbourne (pop. 70,500)
HOTELS: ***Cavendish.* 120 rooms, 94 p.b. ***Grand.* 200 rooms, 200 p.b. **Burlington.* 126 rooms, 73 p.b.
RESTAURANTS: *Le Chantecler,* 7b Bolton Place. *Summer Palace,* Park Gates. Good Chinese food.
Egham (pop. 26,000)
HOTEL: ***Great Fosters.* 23 rooms, 23 p.b. Preserved Tudor house, fine English cooking, not cheap.

114 Britain

Ely (pop. 10,000)
HOTEL: *Lamb.* 26 rooms.
Evesham (pop. 12,000)
HOTELS: **Crown.* 11 rooms, 10 p.b. *Mansion House.* 20 rooms, 3 p.b.
Exeter (pop. 95,000)
27 p.b. Wide variety of food. **Exeter Crest.* 57 rooms, 38 p.b. Motel.
Exmouth (pop. 26,000)
HOTELS: **Devoncourt.* 50 rooms, 18 p.b. **Imperial.* 60 rooms, 22 p.b.
Falmouth (pop. 17,000)
HOTELS: **Falmouth.* 93 rooms, 29 p.b. **Royal Duchy.* 40 rooms, 4 p.b. **Bay.* 40 rooms, 12 p.b.
Ferndown (pop. 4,000, near Wimborne)
HOTEL: ***Dormy.* 83 rooms, 75 p.b. Luxury atmosphere, excellent food.
Folkestone (pop. 45,200)
HOTELS: ***Burlington.* 55 rooms, 40 p.b. ***Grand.* 130 rooms, 49 p.b. **Garden House.* 52 rooms, 12 p.b.
Frinton-on-Sea (pop. 12,000) (near Colchester)
HOTELS: **Frinton Lodge.* 27 rooms, 10 p.b. **Grand.* 44 rooms, 16 p.b.
Glastonbury (pop. 5,000)
HOTELS: **Copper Beech.* 25 rooms, 8 p.b.
Gloucester (pop. 91,000)
HOTELS: **New County.* 33 rooms, 4 p.b. *Fleece.* 38 rooms.
Grange-over-Sands (pop. 3,000)
HOTELS: **Grange,* 36 rooms, 6 p.b. *Grand.* 109 rooms, 18 p.b.
Grasmere (pop. 1,000)
HOTELS: **Prince of Wales.* 32 rooms, 27 p.b. **Swan.* 30 rooms, 2 p.b. *Gold Rill.* (T) 16 rooms, 1 p.b.
Great Yarmouth (pop. 51,000)
HOTELS: ***Carlton.* 103 rooms, 72 p.b. Standard hotel food, not too expensive. *Star.* 35 rooms, 8 p.b.

Interesting inn, good fish.
Grimsby (pop. 95,000)
HOTELS: **Crest.* 134 rooms, 134 p.b. Motel. **Humber Royal.* 57 rooms, 49 p.b. *Ship.* 33 rooms. Good plain hotel cooking, fairly cheap. *Yarborough.* 42 rooms, 6 p.b.
Guildford (pop. 48,000)
HOTELS: **Angel.* 27 rooms, 13 p.b. **White Horse.* 23 rooms, 19 p.b.
Hampton Court
HOTEL: *Greyhound.* 29 rooms, 8 p.b.
Harrogate (pop. 60,000)
HOTELS: ***Majestic*, Ripon Rd. 160 rooms, 120 p.b. **Prospect*, Prospect Pl. 87 rooms, 34 p.b. **St. George*, Ripon Rd. 80 rooms, 12 p.b. Good cooking, moderate prices.
Hastings (and **St. Leonards-on-Sea**) (pop. 65,000)
HOTELS: **Queen's*, Hastings, 120 rooms, 30 p.b. **Royal Victoria*, St. Leonards-on-Sea. 93 rooms, 17 p.b.
Helmsley (pop. 1,600) Near *Rievaulx Abbey*
HOTEL: **Black Swan.* 35 rooms, 30 p.b. Picturesque old inn, good plain cooking.
Henley-on-Thames (pop. 8,000)
HOTELS: *Red Lion.* 22 rooms, 18 p.b. *Sydney House.* 8 rooms. At Nettlebed, near Henley, is the *White Hart Hotel*, well known for its fine food.
Hereford (pop. 46,500)
HOTELS: **Green Dragon.* 80 rooms, 60 p.b. *Castle Pool.* 28 rooms, 2 p.b.
RESTAURANT: *Grey Friars Garden*, Barton St.
Hindhead (pop. 2,500)
HOTELS: *Spaniard Inn.* 6 rooms. *Devil's Punch Bowl.* 15 rooms, 1 p.b.
Honiton (pop. 5,000)
HOTEL: **Deer Park.* 17 rooms, 4 p.b.
Hunstanton (pop. 3,500)

HOTEL: **Golden Lion*. 32 rooms. *Le Strange Arms.* 34 rooms, 8 p.b. Golf links.
Hurley (pop. 1,200)
HOTEL: ****Olde Bell.* 9 rooms, all with p.b. Old luxurious inn, unusually fine food, expensive.
Hythe (pop. 9,000)
HOTEL: ****Imperial.* 81 rooms, 81 p.b.
Ilfracombe (pop. 9,000)
HOTELS: ***Dilkhusa Grand.* 119 rooms, 12 p.b., LC. **Imperial.* 103 rooms, 23 p.b.
Ilkley (pop. 17,200)
HOTELS: ***Craiglands.* 71 rooms, 23 p.b. **Lister's Arms.* 12 rooms.
Ipswich (pop. 120,700)
HOTEL: ***The Great White Horse.* 55 rooms, 7 p.b.
Isle of Man
HOTELS: ***Castletown Golf Links* (in Castletown). 72 rooms, 56 p.b. ***Castle Mona* (in Douglas). 86 rooms, 56 p.b.
Isle of Wight
HOTELS: **Farringford* (in Freshwater). 32 rooms, 12 p.b. A noteworthy restaurant. **Gloster* (in Cowes,) 18 rooms, 10 p.b. **Wheatsheaf* (in Newport). 15 rooms. **Royal Cliff* (in Sandown). 30 rooms, 3 p.b.
Kendal (pop. 18,500)
HOTELS: ***Woolpack.* 17 rooms. ***County.* 10 rooms, 7 p.b.
Kenilworth (pop. 11,000)
HOTELS: ***Chesford Grange.* 39 rooms, 23 p.b.
Keswick (pop. 5,000)
HOTELS: ***Armathwaite Hall* (on Bassenthwaite Lake): 40 rooms, 16 p.b. ***Royal Oak.* 66 rooms, 30 p.b. Good plain food. **Red House.* (LC) 25 rooms, 5 p.b.
Kingsbridge (pop. 3,000)
HOTEL: **King's Arms.* 18 rooms, 2 p.b. **Kingsbridge.* 20 rooms, 20 p.b. Motel.
RESTAURANTS: *Dudley's Brew House,* Union Rd. *Cottage Hotel,* at Hope Cove, is a fine place for seafood—also Devonshire cream.

King's Lynn (pop. 26,000)
HOTEL: ***Duke's Head.* 63 rooms, 51 p.b.
Kirkby Stephen (pop. 1,600)
HOTEL: **King's Arms.* 10 rooms. Old inn.
Lancaster (pop. 47,800)
HOTEL: ***Royal King's Arms.* 60 rooms.
Leamington Spa (pop. 39,000)
HOTELS: ****Manor House.* 55 rooms, 43 p.b. ***Regent.* 85 rooms, 42 p.b.
Leeds (pop. 505,000)
HOTELS: ****Queen's,* City Sq. 202 rooms, all with p.b. ***Parkway.* (Outside of Leeds.) 30 rooms, 6 p.b. Good food. Dancing Saturdays.
RESTAURANT: *Whitelock's Turk's Head,* Briggate. 18th Century inn. *Quebec,* Quebec St. Converted wine cellar.
Leicester (pop. 286,500)
HOTELS: ****Grand.* 142 rooms, 33 p.b. ***Belmont.* 36 rooms, 14 p.b.
RESTAURANTS: *Flamingo.* Conduit St. Cypriot specialties, moderately expensive. *Grand Hotel.* Both restaurant and grill-room recommended.
Leominster (pop. 6,000)
HOTEL: ***Talbot.* 23 rooms, 4 p.b. Good food.
Lichfield (pop. 23,000)
HOTEL: **George.* 35 rooms. 1 p.b. Interesting grill room. **Angel Croft.* 14 rooms.
Lincoln (pop. 70,000)
HOTELS: ****White Hart.* 58 rooms, 33 p.b.
Littlehampton (pop. 17,000)
HOTEL: ***Beach.* 34 rooms, 14 p.b.
Liverpool (pop. 730,000)
HOTELS: ****Adelphi,* Ranelagh Pl. 301 rooms, 119 p.b. ***Lord Nelson,* Lord Nelson St. 70 rooms, 5 p.b.
RESTAURANTS: *Caesar's,* Stanley St. Roman food and flair. *Flynn's,* Old Hall St. Typical.

116 Britain

London

HOTELS: At the head of the list you'll find some of the magnificent de luxe hotels for which London is famous. As hotels in London tend to be more expensive than those in the rest of Britain, you'll find that the prices by which they are categorized are somewhat higher than those of the star categories used in the rest of the fact-finder.

DE LUXE: Elegant and expensive, from about £10 ($24.50) for a single room to £14 ($34.30) and above for a good double.

Claridges, Brook Street, W.1. *Connaught,* Carlos Place, W.1. *Dorchester,* Park Lane, W.1. *Hilton,* Park Lane W.1. *May Fair,* Berkeley St., W.1. *Ritz,* Piccadilly, W.1. *Savoy,* Strand, W.C.2. *Londonderry,* Park Lane, W.1, new.

FIRST CLASS: From about £8 ($19.70) for a single room to doubles from £12 ($29.40).

Athenaeum Court, 116 Piccadilly, W.1. 140 rooms, 140 p.b. *Brown's,* Dover St., W.1. 136 rooms, 92 p.b. *The DeVere,* 1 DeVere Gardens, W.8. 83 rooms, 71 p.b. *Goring,* Grosvenor Gardens, S.W.1. 100 rooms, all with baths. *Mount Royal,* Marble Arch, W.1. 750 rooms, all with baths. *Park Lane,* Piccadilly, W.1. 400 rooms, all with baths. *The Stafford,* 16 St. James's Place. S.W.1. 45 rooms, 40 p.b. *Washington,* Curzon St. W.1. 166 rooms, 127 p.b.

MEDIUM PRICED: From about £6 ($14.70) for a single room to doubles from £10 ($24.50).

Cadogan, 75 Sloane St., S.W.1. 100 rooms, 50 p.b. *Kensington Palace,* DeVere Gardens, W.8. 320 rooms, all with baths. *Quaglino's,* Bury St., S.W.1. 35 rooms, all with baths. *Russell,* Russell Sq., W.C.1. 350 rooms, 180 p.b. *Stratford Court,* 350 Oxford St., W.1. 133 rooms, 133 p.b. *White's,* Lancaster Gate, W.2. 70 rooms, all with baths.

INEXPENSIVE: From about £2 ($4.90) for a single room to doubles from £5 ($12.25). Hotels whose prices are lower than this range are specially noted.

Gore, 189 Queen's Gate, S.W.7. 47 rooms, 31 p.b. *Kensington Close,* Wright's Lane, W.8. 505 rooms, all with baths. A good bargain. *Kensington Gardens,* Kensington Gardens Sq., W.2. 20 rooms. Particularly inexpensive. *Park Court,* 75 Lancaster Gate, W.2. 100 rooms, 89 p.b. Moderately expensive. *Rembrandt,* Thurloe Place, S.W.7. 161 rooms, 73 p.b. *Royal Court,* Sloane Square, S.W.1. 120 rooms, 60 p.b. *Strand Palace,* The Strand, 850 rooms, 550 p.b. W.C.2.

RESTAURANTS: Like hotels, restaurants in London are more expensive than elsewhere in Great Britain.

DE LUXE AND FASHIONABLE: London's most elegant.

The White Tower, 17 Percy St., W.1. *Mirabelle,* 56 Curzon St., W.1. And the fine dining rooms of these hotels: *Claridges, Connaught, May Fair, Ritz,* and *Savoy.*

SOHO: This district is a center of London's nightlife and of fine restaurants.

La Belle Meuniere, 5 Charlotte St., W.1. French. *L'Etoile,* 30 Charlotte St. French and fine English. *Escargot,* 48 Greek St., W.1. French. *Isola Bella,* 15 Frith St., W.1. Italian. *Leoni's Quo Vadis,* 26 Dean St., W.1. Italian. *Schmidt's,* 41 Charlotte St., W.1. German. *Wheelers,* 19 Old Compton St., W.1. The oyster house.

TRADITIONAL: The Roast Beef of Old England (and other truly English fare) at its best.

Cafe Royal, 68 Regent St., W.1. *Cheshire Cheese,* 145 Fleet St., E.C.4. *Cunningham's,* 51 Curzon St., W.1. Famous oyster bar. *Rib Room,* Carlton Tower, Sloane St., S.W.1. *Rule's*

35 Maiden Lane, W.C.2. *Simpson's Tavern*, The Strand, W.C.2.
SOME OF EVERYTHING: International or unusual or just delectable.
Gallery Rendezvous, 55 Beak St., W.1. *Good Earth*, 316–318 King's Road, S.W.3. Chinese. *Khyber Pass*, 21 Bute Street, S.W.7. Indian. *Chanticleer*, Roebuck House, Palace St., S.W.1. Greek and elegant. *Hiroko*, Japanese, 6–8 St. Christopher's Place. W.1. *Elizabethan Room*, Gore Hotel, 189 Queen's Gate, S.W.7. Elizabethan from the rushes on the floor to the wooden plates. *Martinez*, 25 Swallow St., W.1. Genuinely Spanish—fabulous sherries. *Scott's*, 18–20 Coventry St., W.1. Fine shellfish. *Sheekey's Fish Restaurant*, 24 St. Martin's Court, Charing Cross Road.

Looe (pop. 4,000)
HOTELS: **Boscarn*. 27 rooms, 4 p.b. *Punch Bowl Inn* (in Lanreath). 15 rooms, 7 p.b. Fine ancient inn.

Lowestoft (pop. 43,000)
HOTELS: **Victoria*. 53 rooms, 19 p.b. *Harbour*. 11 rooms.

Ludlow (pop. 6,500)
HOTELS: *Angel*. 19 rooms, 2 p.b. *Feathers*. 27 rooms, 6 p.b. Two charming country inns whose restaurants are unusually fine.

Luton (pop. 161,000)
HOTEL: *Cromwell Hotel* at Stevenage, 12 miles from Luton. 16 rooms, 1 p.b. An excellent inn for dining.

Lyme Regis (pop. 3,000)
HOTELS: **High Cliff*. 14 rooms, 2 p.b.

Lynmouth (pop. 450)
HOTELS: **Tors Hotel*. 45 rooms, 8 p.d. Delightful restaurant (salmon, trout, lobster). *Bath*. 26 rooms, 2 p.b.

Lytham St. Annes (pop. 30,000)
HOTELS: ***Clifton Arms*. 43 rooms, 24 p.b. **Grand*. 37 rooms, 9 p.b.

Maidenhead (pop. 45,000)
HOTELS: ***ESSO Motor Hotel*. 195 rooms, 195 p.b. **Bear*. 14 rooms, 14 p.b. **Skindles*. 31 rooms, 26 p.b. Well-known riverside hotel, near London.

Fact Finder 117

Maidstone (pop. 45,000)
HOTEL: ****Great Danes*, 79 rooms, all with bath. **Royal Star*. 40 rooms, 10 p.b. Excellent grill, medium prices.

Malmesbury (pop. 2,500)
HOTEL: **Old Bell*. 22 rooms, 6 p.b. At Tetbury, not far from Malmesbury, you'll find a delightful inn—*The Snooty Fox*. 10 rooms.

Malvern, Great (pop. 22,000)
HOTELS: **Abbey*. 90 rooms, 30 p.b. **Foley Arms*. 29 rooms, 6 p.b.

Manchester (pop. 644,500)
HOTELS: ****Grand*, Aytoun St. 147 rooms, 147 p.b. ****Midland*, Peter St. 324 rooms, 150 p.b. ****Piccadilly*, Piccadilly. 262 rooms, 262 p.b. Brand new, posh.
RESTAURANTS: *Manzil*, 330 Stockport Rd. Indian cuisine. *Vth Inn*, Crown Square, and *Manchester Steakhouse*, 88 Portland St., for hardy fare. *Isola Bella*, Booth Street. The English idea of Italian, not at all bad. *Sinclair's*. Victoria St. Famous sea food restaurant.

Marlow (pop. 6,500)
HOTEL: ****Compleat Angler*. 30 rooms, 30 p.b. Popular luxury inn, lovely situation on river. Fine food.

Melrose (pop. 1,000)
HOTEL: *Burt's*. 19 rooms, 1 p.b.

Monmouth (pop. 5,500)
HOTEL: **Beaufort Arms*. 27 rooms.

Morecambe
HOTELS: **Elms*. 35 rooms, 5 p.b. **Midland*. 38 rooms, 11 p.b.

Moretonhampstead (pop. 1,600)
HOTEL: ****Manor House*. 62 rooms, 41 p.b.

Mousehole (pop. 1,300)
HOTEL: **Lobster Pot*. 28 rooms, 13 p.b. Small picturesque inn, a great variety of superb seafood.

Mullion (pop. 1,000)

HOTEL: **Poldhu*. 42 rooms, 7 p.b.
Newark-on-Trent (pop. 23,000)
HOTEL: *Clinton Arms*. 24 rooms. Plain good cooking.
Newcastle-upon-Tyne (pop. 260,000)
HOTELS: ***Royal Station*, Neville St. 143 rooms, 20 p.b. ***Gosforth Park*, 102 rooms, 102 p.b. ***Royal Turks Head*, 110 rooms, 25 p.b.
RESTAURANTS: *Tilley's*, 10 Northumberland Rd. Fine cuisine and wines. *Bamboo*. Chinese and good.
Newmarket (pop. 10,000)
HOTELS: ***Bedford Lodge*. 10 rooms, 4 p.b. **Rutland Arms*. 34 rooms, 7 p.b.
New Quay (pop. 15,000)
HOTELS: ****Atlantic*. (Easter to October) 50 rooms, 32 p.b. ***Glendorgal*. 36 rooms, 9 p.b. Continental food at moderate prices. ***Headland*. 110 rooms, 56 p.b. Striking Victorian building.
Northampton (pop. 104,000)
HOTELS: ***Westone* (in Weston Favell). 62 rooms, 52 p.b. Good food, moderate prices.
Norwich (pop. 121,000)
HOTELS: ***Castle*. 90 rooms, 12 p.b. Excellent grill room. ***Maid's Head*. 96 rooms, 47 p.b.
RESTAURANTS: *Briton's Arms*, Elm Hill. An old coffee house, for simple meals. *Purdy's*. London West End food at West End prices.
Nottingham (pop. 200,000)
HOTELS: ****Albany*. 160 rooms, 160 p.b. ****Bridgford*. 90 rooms, 90 p.b. Ultra modern. ***George*. 65 rooms, 32 p.b.
RESTAURANTS: *Le Gourmet*, 14 Wheeler Gate. English and continental cuisine. *Trattoria Conti*, 14 St. James St. Obviously, Italian. *Severn's*, 10 Middle Pavement. Old establishment, reliable food, fairly expensive.
Oxford (pop. 105,000)
HOTELS: ***Excelsior Motor Lodge*, Pear Tree Hill Roundabout, 101 rooms, 101 p.b. ****Randolph*, Beaumont St. 114 rooms, 80 p.b. Large and grand. ***Oxford*, Goodstow Road. 100 rooms, 100 p.b. Motel. ***Royal Oxford*, Park End St. 26 rooms, 6 p.b. The dining room is one of the city's better restaurants. **Isis*, Iffley Rd. 42 rooms.
RESTAURANTS: *Elizabethan*, in the Bishop's Palace, St. Aldates Rd. Charming old dining room overlooking college buildings and meadows. Popular with students. Moderately expensive. *La Cantina di Capri*, Cornmarket St. Colorful basement restaurant. *Saraceno*, 15 Magdalen St.

Near Oxford are the *George Hotel*, at Dorchester—fine, thoroughly English specialties: beefsteak, kidney and mushroom pie—and the small town of Thame which has two notable inns, *Spreadeagle*—one of England's most famous, and deserving its reputation for fine food—and *Black Horse*, smaller but boasting an excellent kitchen and wine list.

Paignton (pop. 31,000)
HOTELS: ***Palace*. 59 rooms, 41 p.b. ***Redcliffe*. 75 rooms, 34 p.b.
Penzance (pop. 20,000)
HOTELS: ***Queen's*. 66 rooms, 9 p.b. ***Union*. 30 rooms.
Peterborough (pop. 64,000)
HOTELS: ***Great Northern*. 32 rooms, 5 p.b. **Bull*. 125 rooms, 52 p.b. Well-preserved old building. There is an excellent, moderately expensive restaurant in the *English Garden Hotel* at Norman Cross, not far from Peterborough.
Plymouth (pop. 218,600)
HOTELS: ***Continental*. 73 rooms, 19 p.b. ***Duke of Cornwall*. 73 rooms, 22 p.b. Victorian Gothic at its utmost.
RESTAURANTS: *Crescent Hotel*, Athenaeum St. Excellent grill room, moderately expensive. *Pedro's Octagon*, 69 Union St. Seafood and Cypriot specialties, moderately ex-

pensive. At Yelverton, a few miles inland from Plymouth, the *Moorland Links Hotel* has an unusually fine dining room.
Portsmouth and **Southsea** (pop. 221,000)
HOTELS: **Queen's*, Clarence Parade, Southsea. 87 rooms, 26 p.b. **Royal Beach*, South Parade, Southsea. 101 rooms, 52 p.b. **Keppels*, The Hard, Portsmouth. 20 rooms. Fine restaurant.
RESTAURANTS: *Friar Tuck,* The Strand. Real international (and English) cuisine. *Monck's Bar,* 54 High St. Portsmouth. Sea food and grills. *Murray's,* 27A South Parade, Southsea. Foreign specialties, medium prices. Reserve ahead.
Pulborough (pop. 2,500)
HOTEL: ***Chequers.* 20 rooms, 5 p.b. Fine Scotch dishes in the dining room.
Ripon (pop. 9,500)
HOTELS: ***Spa.* 50 rooms, 10 p.b. ***Unicorn.* 20 rooms, 4 p.b. ***Old Deanery.* Inn with bedrooms available.
Rochester (pop. 45,000)
HOTEL: **King's Head.* 13 rooms.
Ross-on-Wye (pop. 5,400)
HOTELS: ***Pengethley* (in St. Owen's Cross). 18 rooms, 8 p.b. High quality food. ***Royal.* 27 rooms, 2 p.b. **Swan.* 21 rooms.
Rowsley (pop. 350)
HOTEL: ***The Peacock.* 21 rooms, 4 p.b. This delightful country inn features in its dining room rainbow trout from the Wye, roast saddle of lamb, and that most English of "sweets," Bakewell Pudding.
Rugby (pop. 54,000)
HOTEL: ***Three Horse Shoes.* 16 rooms, 12 p.b. Fine dining.
Rye (pop. 4,500)
HOTELS: ***Mermaid Inn.* 20 rooms, 6 p.b. All the best which dining at a fine inn has to offer. **Hope Anchor,* 13 rooms, 2 p.b. Another pleasant inn and another fine dining room.

St. Albans (pop. 51,000)
HOTELS: ***Noke.* 10 rooms, 3 p.b. ***Sopwell House.* 17 rooms, 17 p.b. **White Hart.* 18 rooms, 4 p.b.
St. Ives (pop. 9,000) (Cornwall)
HOTELS: ****Tregenna Castle.* 90 rooms, 38 p.b. ****Chy-an-Drea.* 31 rooms, 31 p.b. ***Porthminster.* 50 rooms, 10 p.b.
St. Ives (pop. 8,700) (Huntingdonshire)
HOTEL: **Golden Lion.* 20 rooms, 4 p.b.
St. Mawes
HOTELS: ****Idle Rocks.* 46 rooms, 15 p.b. ***Tresanton.* 24 rooms, 12 p.b. Overlooking the sea.
Salisbury (pop. 33,500)
HOTELS: **Rose and Crown.* 22 rooms, 15 p.b. **King's Arms Inn.* 17 rooms, 2 p.b. **Red Lion.* 54 rooms, 30 p.b.
Sandwich (pop. 4,400)
HOTEL: ***Bell.* 27 rooms, 12 p.b. Early 19th-century inn.
Scarborough (pop. 44,000)
HOTELS: ****Royal,* St. Nicholas Cliff. 145 rooms, 41 p.b. The fine restaurant features home-cured Yorkshire ham, Scarborough turbot, Flamborough lobsters, and, of course, Yorkshire cheese cakes. ***Grand,* St. Nicholas Cliff. 217 rooms, 66 p.b. ***St. Nicholas,* 120 rooms, 42 p.b.
Scilly Isles (pop. 1,850)
HOTEL: ***The Island.* 30 rooms, 12 p.b. New. Subtropical gardens.
Sevenoaks (pop. 15,000)
HOTEL: **Bligh's.* 14 rooms, 3 p.b.
RESTAURANT: *Le Chantecler.* Fine French food.
Shaftesbury (pop. 3,000)
HOTEL: **Grosvenor.* 48 rooms, 35 p.b.
Sheffield (pop. 500,000)
HOTELS: ****Royal Victoria.* 65 rooms, 19 p.b. ****Hallam Tower.* 136 rooms, 136 p.b. Ultra modern. Overlooks city and countryside.
RESTAURANT: *Dore.* English, French, and Italian dishes.

Britain

Shrewsbury (pop. 51,000)
HOTELS: **Lion*. 60 rooms, 43 p.b.
**Prince Rupert*. 66 rooms, 48 p.b.
The Mytton and Mermaid Hotel, not far from Shrewsbury, has a splendid dining room (try the salmon from the Severn), moderate prices.

Sidmouth (pop. 10,500)
HOTELS: ***Belmont*. 50 rooms, 50 p.b. ****Victoria*. 71 rooms, 71 p.b.

Sonning-on-Thames
HOTEL: *****The French Horn*. Inn. Furnished with English and French antiques. Open fire.

Southampton (pop. 208,000)
HOTELS: ****Polygon*. 119 rooms, 94 p.b. **Royal*. 100 rooms, 7 p.b.

Southport (pop. 84,000)
HOTEL: ****Prince of Wales*. 96 rooms, 36 p.b.

Stamford (pop. 11,000)
HOTEL: ***George*. 50 rooms, 6 p.b.

Stoke-on-Trent (pop. 275,000)
HOTEL: ***North Stafford*. 66 rooms, 66 p.b.

Stratford-upon-Avon (pop. 17,000)
HOTELS: ***Shakespeare*. 70 rooms, 64 p.b. ****Welcombe*. 92 rooms, 81 p.b. ***Alveston Manor*. 129 rooms, 114 p.b. ***Falcon*. 73 rooms, 73 p.b. ***Swan's Nest*. 80 rooms, 45 p.b. ***White Swan*. 60 rooms, 7 p.b. 15th century inn.
RESTAURANT: *Stag's Head,* Alcester Road. English and Italian food.

Stroud (pop. 18,000)
HOTEL: ***Moor Court*. 25 rooms, 2 p.b. Near Stroud, at Amberley. *The Amberley Inn* is a delightful spot for dining.

Sunderland (pop. 181,500)
HOTEL: ***Seaburn*. 57 rooms, 11 p.b.

Swanage (pop. 7,000)
HOTELS: ***Grosvenor*. 150 rooms, 58 p.b. *The Knoll House*, at nearby Studland Bay, has a notable restaurant.

Taunton (pop. 37,000)
HOTEL: ****Castle*. 52 rooms, 16 p.b. Excellent meals, moderately expensive.

Teignmouth (pop. 10,600)
HOTEL: ***Royal*. 90 rooms, 9 p.b.

Tewkesbury (pop. 5,000)
HOTEL: **Royal Hop Pole*. 25 rooms, 10 p.b.

Tintagel (pop. 650)
HOTEL: **Wharncliffe Arms*. 21 rooms.

Tintern (pop. 750)
HOTEL: **Beaufort*. 27 rooms, 8 p.b.

Torquay (pop. 53,000)
HOTELS: *****Imperial,* Park Hill Rd. 165 rooms, 165 p.b. ****Osborne*. 100 rooms, 72 p.b. ****Victoria*. 61 rooms, 31 p.b.
RESTAURANT: *Regency*, 28 Torwood St. Fish specialties. Medium prices.

Truro (pop. 13,000)
HOTEL: **Carlton*. 19 rooms, 2 p.b.
RESTAURANTS: *Rendezvous des Gourmets*. Continental. At Portloe, nearby, the *Lugger Hotel* is an excellent inn—Cornish pasties and seafood.

Tunbridge Wells (pop. 39,000)
HOTELS: ***Calverley*. 50 rooms, 16 p.b. ***Spa*. 80 rooms, 14 p.b.
RESTAURANT: *High Rocks*. Creeper-covered inn at High Rocks.

Uttoxeter (pop. 7,500)
HOTEL: ***White Hart*. 12 rooms, 10 p.b. A handsome old inn with a fine kitchen. Try the grilled gammon and peaches. Moderately priced.

Veryan (pop. 900)
HOTEL: ****Nare*. 50 rooms. 5 p.b. Beautifully situated hotel, luxurious atmosphere.

Wantage (pop. 7,300)
HOTEL: **Bear*. 17 rooms. Authentic old inn.

Warminster (pop. 10,500)
HOTEL: **Old Bell*. 11 rooms, 3 p.b. Attractive old inn, good food, not expensive.

Warwick (pop. 15,600)
HOTELS: **Lord Leycester*. 50 rooms, 8 p.b. **Woolpack*. 29 rooms, 2 p.b.

Good food at low prices.
RESTAURANT: *Saxon Mill*, Guy's Cliffe. Reconverted old mill.
Wells (pop. 6,000)
HOTELS: **Crown*. 10 rooms, 4 p.b. Good kitchen, moderate prices. **Swan*. 25 rooms, 1 p.b. Sheringham lobsters and Blakeney mussels, in season, are the specialties of the fine restaurant at the *Blakeney Hotel*, at Blakeney, not far from Wells.
Winchester (pop. 30,000)
HOTELS: ****Wessex*. 91 rooms, 91 p.b. ***Royal*. 40 rooms, 5 p.b. **Southgate*. 14 rooms.
RESTAURANTS: *Georgian*, 29 Jury St. *Elizabethan*, 18-19 Jewry St. Historic setting for good food and wine.
Windermere (pop. 6,000)
HOTELS: ***Belsfield*, 60 rooms, 21 p.b. ***Langdale Chase*. 40 rooms, 18 p.b. Delightful location and one of the Lake District's best restaurants.
RESTAURANTS: *Old England Hotel*, at Bowness-on-Windermere. All the lakeland specialties: salmon and trout, splendid roast venison, goose or duck. *John Peel Inn*, fine *table d'hote*.
Windsor (pop. 29,000)
HOTEL: ***Old House*. 40 rooms, 16 p.b.
Woburn Sands (pop. 1,400)
HOTEL: **Swan*. 12 rooms.
Worcester (pop. 62,600)
HOTELS: ***Star*. 38 rooms, 6 p.b.
Worksop (pop. 31,000)
HOTELS: **Royal*. 11 rooms. **Lion*. 12 rooms. Coaching inn.
Worthing (pop. 70,000)
HOTELS: ***Beach*. 81 rooms, 32 p.b.
York (pop. 105,000)
HOTELS: ****Royal Station*. 119 rooms, 64 p.b. ****Viking*. 106 rooms, 106 p.b. ***Chase*. 55 rooms, 22 p.b.

SCOTLAND

Aberdeen (pop. 183,000)
HOTELS: ****Station*. 63 rooms. 13 p.b. ***Caldonian*, Union Terrace. 61 rooms, 48 p.b. ***Northern*, Great Northern Road. 34 rooms, 4 p.b. Modern, good food and service. ***Dee*, Garthdee Road. 44 rooms, 44 p.b. Motel.
RESTAURANT: *Royal Athenaeum*, 7 Union St.
Aberfoyle (pop. 1,150)
HOTELS: ***Convenanter's Inn*, 43 rooms, 28 p.b. Old country inn.
Aboyne (pop. 2,200)
HOTELS: ***Birse Lodge*. 19 rooms, 8 p.b. **Huntly Arms*. 56 rooms, 4 p.b. 4 p.b.
Alloway (pop. 1,000)
HOTEL: **Burns Monument*. 7 rooms.
Arran, Isle of
HOTELS: ***Douglas* (Brodick). 49 rooms, 8 p.b. **Kildonan* (Kildonan). 30 rooms. **Whiting Bay*. 20 rooms.
Ayr (pop. 43,000)
HOTELS: ***Station*. 70 rooms, 20 p.b. **Elms Court*. 20 rooms. **County*. 33 rooms, 2 p.b.
Ballachulish (pop. 1,200)
HOTEL: ***Ballachulish*. 41 rooms, 6 p.b.
Ballater (pop. 1,300)
HOTELS: ***Craigendarroch*. 34 rooms, 17 p.b. ***Loirston*. 40 rooms, 4 p.b., T.
Balloch (pop. 2,500)
HOTELS: ***Loch Lomond*. 48 rooms, 5 p.b.
Banchory (pop. 2,500)
HOTELS: ***Raemoir*. 25 rooms, 7 p.b. ***Tor-na Coille*. 32 rooms, 4 p.b.
Braemar (pop. 500)
HOTEL: ***Invercauld Arms*. 55 rooms, 12 p.b. Good hotel cooking.
Bridge of Allan (pop. 3,200)
HOTEL: ***Allan Water*. 54 rooms, 3 p.b.
Brora (pop. 1,800)
HOTELS: ***Royal Marine*. 24 rooms. **Sutherland Arms*. 13 rooms. Attractive atmosphere, good food.
Bute, Isle of
HOTEL: ****Glenburn* (in Rothesay). 97 rooms, 27 p.b.
Connel Ferry (pop. 280)
HOTEL: **Falls of Lora*. 29 rooms.

122 Britain

Dornoch (pop. 790)
Hotel: **Royal Golf.* 33 rooms, 16 p.b.

Drymen (pop. 1,214)
Hotel: **Buchanan Arms.* 26 rooms, 6 p.b. Celebrated, especially for curries.

Dumfries (pop. 19,000)
Hotels: **Cairndale.* 40 rooms, 7 p.b. High quality meals, not expensive. **Station.* 28 rooms, 10 p.b.

Dundee (pop. 177,000)
Hotels: **Angus.* 60 rooms, 60 p.b. New. **Royal.* 82 rooms, 7 p.b. **Invercarse.* 28 rooms, 4 p.b.

Dunfermline (pop. 44,700)
Hotel: *Brucefield,* 9 rooms, 3 p.b.

Edinburgh (pop. 473,000)
Hotels: ***Caledonian,* Princes St. 223 rooms, 196 p.b. ***ESSO.* 120 rooms, 120 p.b. Motel. ***George.* 185 rooms, 185 p.b. ***North British.* 131 rooms, 131 p.b. **Carlton.* 92 rooms, 92 p.b. **Fox Covert.* 50 rooms, 43 p.b. **Roxburghe.* 75 rooms, 60 p.b.
Restaurants: *Prestonfield House,* Prestonfield Road. Elegant house dating from 1735. *Cafe Royal,* 17 West Register St. *Oratava,* 41 Craigmillar Park, Newington. *Crammond Inn,* Crammond Village. Secluded village setting. *Beehive Inn,* Grassmarket. Old established restaurant, good food, fairly expensive. *Doric Tavern,* 15 Market St. Good classical menu, medium prices. *Handsel,* 22 Stafford St. Excellent food, Swedish specialties, fairly inexpensive.

Elgin (pop. 10,500)
Hotel: *Gordon Arms.* 26 rooms. Good plain Scottish cooking. On the main road between Inverness and Aberdeen.

Fort William (pop. 2,600)
Hotels: ***Clan MacDuff.* 46 rooms, 24 p.b. *Alexandra.* 34 rooms, 4 p.b. *Grand.* 35 rooms, 10 p.b. ***Royal Stuart.* 107 rooms, 68 p.b.

Gatehouse-of-Fleet (pop. 900)
Hotel: **Cally.* 77 rooms, 19 p.b.

Glasgow (pop. 1,100,000)
Hotels: ***Central,* Gordon St. 248 rooms, 87 p.b. ***Lorne,* 923 Sauchiehall St. 87 rooms, 87 p.b. ***St. Enoch.* 147 rooms, 147 p.b. **Bellahouston.* 46 rooms, 46 p.b. **Stepps.* 50 rooms, 16 p.b. **More's.* 66 rooms, 12 p.b. *Grosvenor.* 100 rooms, 100 p.b.
Restaurants: *Ferrari,* 10 Sauchiehall St. Good Italian cooking, medium prices, large choice of wines. *Adriano,* Beacons Hotel, 7 Park Terrace. Bands and dancing. *Ambassador,* 19 Blysthwood Square. Dancing. *Danish Food Centre,* 56 St. Vincent St. *Vesuvio,* 15 St. Vincent Place. *Guy's,* 196 Hope St. Excellent cuisine. *One-O-One,* 101 Hope St. First-class, near theaters. *Whitehall,* 51 W. Regent St. Businessmen's hangout.

Glencoe (pop. 1,100)
Hotel: *Glencoe.* 17 rooms.

Gleneagles (pop. 500)
Hotels: ***Gleneagles.* 210 rooms, 210 p.b. *Castle* (in Glendevon). 30 rooms, 3 p.b.

Golspie (pop. 1,300)
Hotel: **Sutherland Arms.* 19 rooms, 2 p.b.

Inverness (pop. 28,000)
Hotels: ***Station.* 75 rooms, 20 p.b. Good food, fairly expensive. **Douglas.* 88 rooms.

Inversnaid (On Loch Lomond)
Hotel: *Inversnaid.* 41 rooms. On the east side of Loch Lomond.

Jedburgh
Hotels: *Royal.* 7 rooms.

Kelso (pop. 4,100)
Hotel: **Ednam House.* 34 rooms, 16 p.b.

Kinloch Rannoch (pop. 200)
Hotel: *Dunalastair.* 20 rooms. At the eastern end of the loch.

Kirkcudbright (pop. 3,500)
Hotel: **Selkirk.* 17 rooms, 2 p.b. Good Scottish country cooking. In the heart of the western lowlands.

Kirriemuir (pop. 3,500)
Hotel: **Airlie Arms.* 8 rooms. The town is the birthplace of James M. Barrie.

Kyle of Lochalsh (pop. 1,650)
Hotel: ****Lochalsh.* 36 rooms, 5 p.b.

Largs (pop. 8,600)
Hotels: ***Castle.* 21 rooms, 1 p.b. ***Marine and Curlinghall.* 90 rooms, 14 p.b. On the Firth of Clyde.

Lasswade (near Edinburgh)
Hotel: **Melville Castle.* 21 rooms, 1 p.b. Near Roslin Castle.

Luss (pop. 495, on Loch Lomond)
Hotel: **Inverberg.* 12 rooms.

North Berwick (pop. 4,000)
Hotel: **Blenheim House.* 12 rooms, 3 p.b.

Oban (pop. 6,200)
Hotels: ***Park.* 85 rooms, 18 p.b. ***Alexandra.* 62 rooms, 20 p.b. Center for touring the western isles.

Orkney Islands (pop. 21,250)
Hotels: **Kirkwall.* 46 rooms. **Stromness.* 47 rooms.

Peebles
Hotels: ****Peebles Hydro.* 150 rooms, 50 p.b. **Cross Keep.* 14 rooms, 2 p.b.

Perth (pop. 40,500)
Hotels: ***Royal George.* 52 rooms. Discriminating food at medium prices. ***Station.* 55 rooms, 20 p.b.

Portsonachan
Hotel: ***Portsonachan.* 26 rooms. First-rate hotel, discriminating and varied menu. Eleven miles from Inverary Castle.

Prestwick (pop. 11,400)
Hotel: **Towans* (Prestwick Airport), 42 rooms, 7 p.b.

St. Andrews (pop. 9,500)
Hotels: ***Scores,* 34 rooms, 8 p.b. ***Rusack's,* 72 rooms, 19 p.b. **Station and Windsor,* 41 rooms.

St. Boswells (pop. 1,200)
Hotel: **Dryburgh Abbey.* 34 rooms, 12 p.b.

Selkirk (pop. 6,000)
Hotels: ***Woodburn.* 5 rooms, 1 p.b. **County.* 7 rooms.

Shetland Isles (pop. 19,500)
Hotel: **Grand* (in Lerwick). 25 rooms.

Skye, Isle of (pop. 12,500)
Hotels: ***Royal* (in Portree). 28 rooms, 8 p.b. **King's Arms* (in Kyleakin). 23 rooms. **Marine.* 28 rooms.

Stirling (pop. 27,000)
Hotel: ***Golden Lion.* 85 rooms, 16 p.b. Distinctive food.

Turnberry
Hotel: ****Turnberry.* 120 rooms, 120 p.b. Famous golf course. Near Culzean Castle.

WALES

Aberdaron (pop. 1,000)
Hotel: **Ty Newydd Hotel.* 17 rooms. Quiet hotel, good food.

Aberdovey (pop. 1,000)
Hotels: ***Trefiddian.* 47 rooms, 30 p.b. ***Penhelig Arms.* 6 rooms, 2 p.b.

Abersoch
Hotel: **Porth Tocym.* 28 rooms, 5 p.b. (LC) Small hotel. Imaginative cooking.

Aberystwyth (pop. 9,500)
Hotels: ***Belle Ville.* 50 rooms, 11 p.b. ***Conrah.* 10 rooms, 4 p.b. **Talbot.* 16 rooms.

Bala (pop. 1,500)
Hotel: ****White Lion Royal.* 26 rooms, 2 p.b. Old hotel with atmosphere. Good plain cooking.

Bangor (pop. 14,000)
Hotel: ***Waverly.* 15 rooms.

Barmouth (pop. 2,500)
Hotels: **Min-y-Mor.* (T) 60 rooms, 4 p.b. **Hendre Mynach,* 12 rooms, 2 p.b.

Beaumaris, Isle of Anglesey (pop. 2,100)
Hotel: **Old Bull's Head.* 15 rooms, 4 p.b. 17th-century inn, good food at medium prices.

"The Old Siege House"

Beddgelert (pop. 400)
HOTELS: *Tanronen*, 10 rooms, 2 p.b. *Saracen's Head*. 13 rooms, 6 p.b.
Betws-y-Coed (pop. 750)
HOTELS: *Glan Alber*, 22 rooms, 4 p.b. *Royal Oak*. 34 rooms, 1 p.b.
Builth Wells (pop. 1,700)
HOTEL: *Greyhound*. 13 rooms.
Caernarvon (pop. 9,200)
HOTEL: *Royal*. 44 rooms, 3 p.b.
Capel Curig (pop. 400)
HOTEL: *Tyn-y-Coed*. 11 rooms. Large well-cooked dinners.
Cardiff (pop. 244,000)
HOTELS: ***Angel*. 111 rooms, 75 p.b. **Park*. 105 rooms, 80 p.b. **Royal*. 79 rooms, 12 p.b.
Conway (pop. 10,200)
HOTEL: *Castle*. 26 rooms, 1 p.b.
Criccieth (pop. 1,550)
HOTELS: **Bron Eifion*. 19 rooms, 7 p.b. **George IV*. 47 rooms, 4 p.b.
Dolgellau (pop. 2,250)
HOTEL: **Golden Lion Royal*. 30 rooms, 4 p.b.
Ganllwyd (pop. 150)
HOTEL: *Tyn-y-Groes*. 12 rooms. Simple, good food.
Harlech (pop. 1,000)
HOTEL: *St. David's*. 73 rooms, 6 p.b.
Llandrindod Wells (pop. 3,000)
HOTELS: **Glen Usk*. 88 rooms, 32 p.b. **Metropole*. 138 rooms, 60 p.b.
Llandudno (pop. 16,700)
HOTELS: ***Grand*. 120 rooms, 36 p.b. **Imperial*. 121 rooms, 37 p.b. Good restaurant.
Llangollen (pop. 3,200)
HOTEL: *Royal*. 32 rooms, 9 p.b.
Llanwrtyd Wells (pop. 560)
HOTEL: **Abernant Lake*, 44 rooms, 12 p.b.
Milford Haven (pop. 12,000)
HOTEL: *Lord Nelson*. 30 rooms, 7 p.b.
Pembroke (pop. 12,300)
HOTELS: **Lion*. 33 rooms. *Old King's Arms*. 16 rooms, 13 p.b.
Penrhyndeudraeth (pop. 1,800)
HOTEL: ***Portmeirion*. 74 rooms, 24 p.b.
Porthcawl (pop. 14,000)
HOTELS: ***Seabank*. 93 rooms, 29 p.b. **Esplanade*. 80 rooms, 27 p.b.
Prestatyn (pop. 9,000)
HOTEL: *Nant Hall*. 18 rooms, 18 p.b.
Rhyl (pop. 21,500)
HOTEL: **Westminster*. 40 rooms, 2 p.b. Good, varied menu.
Tenby (pop. 5,000)
HOTELS: **Belgrave*. 42 rooms, 22 p.b. **Imperial*. 50 rooms, 20 p.b. *Coburg*. 30 rooms, 5 p.b. Old-fashioned.
Welshpool (pop. 6,000)
HOTEL: *Royal Oak*. 23 rooms. Old inn.

INDEX

Aberdaron, 123
Aberdeen, 97, 121
Aberdovey, 123
Aberfoyle, 121
Abersoch, 123
Aberystwyth, 103–4, 123
Abingdon, 110
Aboyne, 97–98, 121
Addresses, 44
Air travel, 27, 31
Alfriston, 63, 110
Alloway, 121
Alton, 110
Ambleside, 110
Amersham, 110
Amesbury, 110
Ampthill, 110
Anglesey, 105
Arran, Isle of, 95, 121
Arundel, 64, 110
Ascot, 110
Aston Clinton, 110
Austen, Jane, 65
Automobiles, 31, 44, 47
Aylesbury, 110
Ayr, 94–95, 121

Bagshot, 110
Bala, 123
Ballaculish, 121
Ballater, 98, 121
Ballet, 38
Balloch, 121
Bamburgh, 87, 110
Banbury, 78, 110
Banchory, 97, 121
Bangor, 106, 123
Barmouth, 123
Barnstaple, 71, 110
Bath, 67–68, 111
Battle, 111
Beaumaris, 105, 123
Beddgelert, 106, 124
Bedford, 78, 111
Berwick - upon - Tweed, 111
Betws-y-Coed, 106, 124
Bexhill-on-Sea, 111
Birmingham, 76, 111
Blackpool, 111
Blair Atholl, 98

Bodinnick, 111
Bodnant Gardens, 106
Bognor Regis, 111
Borrowdale, 111
Boston, 79, 111
Bournemouth, 66, 111
Bourton-on-the-Water, 111
Bovey Tracey, 111
Bradford, 111
Braemar, 98, 121
Breconshire, 103
Bridge of Allan, 121
Bridport, 111
Brighton, 64, 111
Bristol, 68, 112
British Museum, 57
Brixham, 112
Broadstairs, 112
Broadway, 75, 112
Brockenhurst, 112
Brontë family, 81
Brora, 121
Bryn-Englwys, 107
Builth Wells, 124
Burford, 112
Burns, Robert, 94–95
Bury St. Edmunds, 73, 112
Buses, 31, 32
Bute, Isle of, 121
Butler, Lady Eleanor, 107
Buxton, 112
Byron, George Lord, 78

Caernarvon, 106, 124
Caerphilly, 102
Cambridge, 72, 112
Canterbury, 62–63, 112
Capel Curig, 106, 124
Cardiff, 101, 124
Cardiganshire, 103–4
Carlisle, 86, 112
Carlyle, Thomas, 55–56
Carmarthen Valley, 102
Carnaby Street, 42
Carnegie, Andrew, 95
Castles
  Allington, 61–62
  Balmoral, 98

  Carisbrooke, 66
  Chirk, 107
  Crathes, 97
  Edward I, 105
  Glamis, 96
  Merewroth, 62
  Penrhyn, 106
  Portchester, 66
  Powis, 107
  Rosslyn, 94
  St. Fagan's, 102
  St. Michael's Mt., 70–71
  Stokesay, 78
  Warwick, 76
  Windsor, 74
  (*See also* by towns)
Cerne Abbas, 69
Chagford, 112
Changing of the Guard, 56
Charles II, 19, 59, 77
Cheddar, 68, 112
Cheltenham, 39, 112
Cheshire County, 78
Chester, 78, 113
Chesterfield, 113
Chichester, 64, 113
Chiddingfold, 61, 113
Chipping Camden, 113
Chipping Norton, 113
Chipping Sodbury, 113
Christ in Majesty, 102
Church Stretton, 113
Churches, Cathedrals, etc.
  King's College, 72
  Llandaff, 101
  St. David's, 102–3
  St. Giles, 92
  St. Machar, 97
  St. Margaret's, 53
  St. Mary Redcliffe, 68
  St. Michael's Mt., 70–71
  St. Paul's, 51
  St. Wilfred, 82
  Westminster Abbey, 53–54
  (*See also* by towns)
Cirencester, 75, 113

125

Clevedon, 113
Clothes, 27, 42
Clovelly, 71, 113
Cobham, 61
Cockermouth, 86
Colchester, 73, 113
Coniston, 85
Connel, 121
Conway, 106, 124
Cornwall, 70–71
Costs, 25–26
Cotswolds, The, 75
Coventry, 76, 113
Criccieth, 105, 124
Cricket, 39–40
Cromer, 113
Culbone, 68–69
Customs regulations, 27

Dartmoor, 70
Dartmouth, 70, 113
Derby, 113
Derbyshire, 79
Devon, 69
Dickens, Charles, 56, 61
Disraeli, Benjamin, 59
Do's and Don't's, 47
Dolgelley, 105, 124
Doncaster, 113
Dorchester, 69
Dorking, 60, 113
Dornoch, 122
Dorset, 69
Dovedale, 113
Dover, 63, 113
Drinking, 34, 35, 37
Droitwich Spa, 113
Dryburgh Abbey, 90–91
Drymen, 122
Dumfries, 94–95, 122
Dundee, 96, 122
Dunfermline, 95, 122
Durham, 86–87, 113

East Anglia, 72–74
Eastbourne, 113
East Riding, 81
Edinburgh, 38, 91–94, 122
Edward I, 16, 105, 106
Edward II, 75, 106
Egham (island), 74, 113
Electric current, 43
Elgin, 122

Elgin Marbles, 57
Elizabeth I, 17–18, 59, 68
Ely, 72–73, 114
England, 49–87, 110–21
Epstein, Jacob, 102
Etiquette, 46
Eton, 74
Evesham, 114
Exeter, 69–70, 114
Exmouth, 114

Falmouth, 70, 114
Farne (islands), 87
Ferndown, 114
Fishing, 40–41
Folkestone, 114
Food, 34–37
Fort Augustus, 99
Fort William, 98–99, 122
Frinton-on-Sea, 114

Ganllwyd, 124
Gardens, 41
Gatehouse-of-Fleet, 122
Glasgow, 94, 122
Glastonbury, 68, 114
Glencoe, 98
Gleneagles, 122
Glenmoriston, 122
Gloucester, 75, 114
Glyndebourne, 39, 63
Godalming, 61
Golf, 40
Golspie, 122
Gower, 102
Grange-over-Sands, 114
Grasmere, 114
Great Yarmouth, 73, 114
Greenwich, 59
Grimsby, 114
Guildford, 60, 114
Guildhall, 56

Hampshire, 65
Hampton Court, 58, 114
Harlech, 105, 124
Harrogate, 81–82, 114
Hastings, 63, 114
Haverfordwest, 102
Hawick, 90
Hawkshead, 85
Haworth, 81
Hebrides, 99

Helmsley, 114
Henley-on-Thames, 114
Henry V, 17, 66
Henry VIII, 17
Hereford, 77, 114
Hever, 62
Hindhead, 114
Holbein, Hans, 74
Holidays, 43
Honiton, 114
Horse Guards, 56
Hotels, 29–30, 32–33 109 ff.
Houses, historic, 41
  Blickling Hall, 73–74
  Boughton Monchelsea Place, 62
  Bowes Museum, 87
  Chatsworth, 79
  Chiswick House, 58
  Fountains Hall, 82
  Goodwood House, 64–65
  Ham House, 58
  Harewood House, 82
  Hatfield House, 59
  Holkham Hall, 74
  Hopetoun House, 94
  Houghton Tower, 83–84
  Hughenden Manor, 59
  Knole, 62
  Levens Hall, 85
  Loseley House, 60
  Mansion House, 57
  Newby Hall, 83
  Penshurst Place, 62
  Petworth House, 64
  Plas Mawr, 106
  Plas Newydd, 105, 107
  Rudding Park, 82
  Seaton Delaval Hall, 87
  Sulgrave Manor, 78
  Wilton House, 67
  (See also famous owners)
Hull, 81
Hunstanton, 115
Hurley, 115
Hythe, 115

Ilfracombe, 115
Ilkley, 115

Inns, 33–34
Inns of Court, 55
Inveraray, 98
Inverness, 99, 122
Inversnaid, 122
Iona (island), 98
Ipswich, 73, 115

Jedburgh, 90, 122
Johnson, Samuel, 56, 76

Keats, John, 56
Kelso, 90, 122
Kendal, 84, 115
Kenilworth, 47, 115
Kent, 61
Keswick, 85, 115
Kew Gardens, 58
Kingsbridge, 115
King's Lynn, 115
Kinloch Rannoch, 122
Kipling, Rudyard, 64
Kirkby Stephen, 115
Kirkcudbright, 122
Kirriemuir, 122–23
Knaresborough, 82
Knox, John, 92–93, 96
Kyle of Lochalsh, 123

Lake District (Eng.), 84–86
Lancashire, 83–84
Lancaster, 83, 115
Largs, 123
Lasswade, 122
Leamington Spa, 115
Leconfeld Aphrodite, 64
Leeds, 115
Leicester, 78, 115
Leominster, 115
Leuchars, 96
Lewes, 64
Lichfield, 76, 115
Lincoln, 79, 115
Lindisfarne, 87
Littlehampton, 115
Liverpool, 83, 115
Llandrindod, 103, 124
Llandudno, 104, 124
Llanfair P. G., 105
Llangollen, 107, 124
Llanwrtyd Wells, 124
London, 32, 50–58, 116
Looe, 117

Lowestoft, 117
Ludlow, 77, 117
Luss, 122
Luton, 117
Lyme Regis, 69, 117
Lynmouth, 71, 117
Lynton, 71
Lytham St. Annes, 117

Magazines, 45
Maidenhead, 117
Maidstone, 61–62, 117
Malvern, Great, 117
Man, Isle of, 84, 115
Manchester, 83, 117
Marlow, 117
Mary of Scotland, 90, 92
Medical requirements, 26
Melrose, 117
Midlands, 74–79
Milford Haven, 102, 124
Money, 28–29
Monmouth, 77, 117
Morecambe, 117
Moreton Hampstead, 117
Mousehole, 117
Mullion, 117
Museums (London), 57–58
Music, 38–39

National Gallery, 57
National Portrait Gallery, 58
Newark-on-Trent, 118
Newcastle, 87, 118
New Forest, 66
Newmarket, 73, 118
Newquay, 118
Newspapers, 45
Northampton, 118
North Berwick, 122
North Devon, 71
North Riding, 83
Northumberland, 87
Norwich, 73, 118
Nottingham, 78, 118

Oban, 98, 122
Old Bailey, 57
Old Cheshire Cheese, 57
Orkney Islands, 122
Oxford, 74–75, 118

Paignton, 118

Palaces
  Banqueting Hall (Whitehall), 53
  Blenheim, 41, 75
  Buckingham, 52, 56
  Holyrood, 93
  Kensington, 55
  Kew, 58
  Linlithgow, 94
  St. James, 52, 56
Parliament, 56
Passports, 26, 47
Peebles, 91, 122
Pembroke, 102, 124
Pembrokeshire, 102
Penrhyndeudraeth, 124
Penzance, 71, 118
Perth, 96, 122
Peterborough, 118
Plymouth, 70, 118
Polperro, 70
Ponsonby, Hon. Sarah, 107
Porthcawl, 124
Portmadoc, 105
Portsmouth, 66, 119
Portsonachan, 122
Post Office Tower, 57
Postal service, 43–44
Praxiteles, 64
Prestatyn, 124
Prestbury, 119
Prestwick, 122
Pubs, 30, 33–34
Pulborough, 119

Queen's Guard, 56

Racing, 40
Radnorshire, 103
Railroads, 31
Restaurants, 109 ff.
Rhyl, 106–7, 124
Richmond, 58
Ripon, 82, 119
Robin Hood, 78
Rochester, 61, 119
Roman Empire, 13–14
Ross-on-Wye, 77, 119
Rowsley, 79
Royal Albert Hall, 57
Royal Tunbridge Wells, 62
Rugby (game), 39
Rugby (town), 119

127

Ruskin, John, 85
Rye, 63, 119

Sackville-West family, 62
St. Albans, 59, 119
St. Andrews, 96, 122
St. Asaph, 107
St. Boswells, 122
St. Ives, 71, 119
St. Mawes, 119
Salisbury, 67, 119
Sandwich, 119
Scarborough, 83, 119
Scilly Islands, 71, 119
Scotland, 89–99, 121–23
Scott, Sir Walter, 90–91
Selkirk, 122
Sevenoaks, 62, 119
Shaftesbury, 69, 119
Shakespeare, William, 76
Sheffield, 119
Sherwood Forest, 78
Shetland Isles, 122
Ships, 27
Shopping, 42–43
Shrewsbury, 78, 120
Shropshire, 77
Sidmouth, 120
Skye, Isle of, 99, 123
Soane's Museum, 58
Soccer, 39
Somerset, 67
Sonning-on-Thames, 120
Southampton, 65, 120
Southey, Robert, 86
Southport, 120
Sports, 39–41

Stamford, 120
Stevenson, R. L., 91, 93
Stirling, 95–96, 123
Stoke-on-Trent, 120
Stonehenge, 67
Stratford-on-Avon, 76, 120
Stroud, 120
Subways, 32
Sunderland, 120
Surrey, 60
Sussex, 63
Swanage, 69, 120

Tate Gallery, 58
Taunton, 120
Taxis, 30, 32
Teignmouth, 120
Telegraph service, 43
Telephones, 44
Tenby, 102, 124
Tewkesbury, 75, 120
Theater, 30, 37–38
Tintagel, 71, 120
Tintern, 120
Tipping, 29–30
Torquay, 70, 120
Tower of London, 57
Travelers Checks, 29, 47
Trooping the Colour, 57
Truro, 120
Tunbridge Wells, 120
Turnberry, 123
Tussaud's, 57

Uttoxeter, 120

Vaccinations, 26
Valle Crucis Abbey, 107
Van Dyck, Anthony, 67, 74
Veryn, 120
Victoria, Queen, 22

Wales, 100–7, 123–24
Wallace Collection, 58
Wantage, 120
Warminster, 120
Warwick, 120
Weather, 26
Wells, 68, 121
Welshpool, 124
West Riding, 81
Whitby, 83
Wight, Isle of, 65–66, 115
William of Normandy, 15
Wiltshire, 67
Winchester, 65, 121
Windermere, 121
Windsor, 74, 121
Wines, 37
Witt, Jacob de, 93
Woburn, 121
Worcester, 77, 120
Wordsworth, William, 85
Worksop, 121
Worthing, 121

York, 80–81, 121